Unchecked and Unbalanced

HOOVER STUDIES IN POLITICS, ECONOMICS, AND SOCIETY

General Editors
Peter Berkowitz and Tod Lindberg

Unchecked and Unbalanced

How the Discrepancy Between
Knowledge and Power Caused the
Financial Crisis and Threatens Democracy

Arnold Kling

HOOVER STUDIES
IN POLITICS, ECONOMICS,
AND SOCIETY

Published in cooperation with
HOOVER INSTITUTION
Stanford University • Stanford, California

ROWMAN & LITTLEFIELD PUBLISHERS, INC.
Lanham • Boulder • New York • Toronto • Plymouth, UK

ROWMAN & LITTLEFIELD PUBLISHERS, INC.

THE HOOVER INSTITUTION ON WAR, REVOLUTION AND PEACE, founded at Stanford University in 1919 by Herbert Hoover, who went on to become the thirty-first president of the United States, is an interdisciplinary research center for advanced study on domestic and international affairs. The views expressed in its publications are entirely those of the authors and do not necessarily reflect the views of the staff, officers, or Board of Overseers of the Hoover Institution.

www.hoover.org

Published in the United States of America by Rowman & Littlefield Publishers, Inc.
A wholly owned subsidiary of The Rowman & Littlefield Publishing Group, Inc.
4501 Forbes Boulevard, Suite 200, Lanham, Maryland 20706
www.rowmanlittlefield.com
Estover Road
Plymouth PL6 7PY
United Kingdom
Distributed by National Book Network

Copyright © 2010 by the Board of Trustees of the Leland Stanford Junior University

Published in cooperation with the Hoover Institution at Stanford University.

First printing, 2010
16 15 14 13 12 11 10 09   9 8 7 6 5 4 3 2 1
Manufactured in the United States of America

British Library Cataloguing in Publication Information Available

Library of Congress Cataloging-in-Publication Data Available

ISBN: 978-1-4422-0124-8 (cloth : alk. paper)
ISBN: 978-1-4422-0126-2 (electronic)

♾ The paper used in this publication meets the minimum requirements of American National Standard for Information Sciences—Permanence of Paper for Printed Library Materials, ANSI/NISO Z39.48-1992.

I would like to dedicate this book to my late father, Merle Kling, who first introduced me to political science. This would be a much better book had he been alive to comment while I was writing it.

Contents

Preface

This book represents an attempt to explore the problem of the discrepancy between the trends in two phenomena: *knowledge* is becoming more diffuse, while political *power* is becoming more concentrated. The first part of the book looks at the financial crisis of 2008 as an illustration of the knowledge/power discrepancy. The second part looks at broader indicators of the diffusion of knowledge and the concentration of power. The third part suggests reforms that could promote the provision of public goods using mechanisms that would provide for greater equality of political power and help to alleviate the knowledge/power discrepancy.

What are the lessons of the financial crisis that emerged in 2008? One popular narrative claims that bankers and financial markets engaged in rampant misbehavior, demonstrating a need for closer regulatory supervision. However, the interpretation I offer is quite different. In this alternate view, financial industry executives and regulatory officials lacked the ability to fathom the complexity of the system that had emerged. As a result, they did not foresee the consequences of what were, from their perspective, sound, rational decisions. If the response to this failure is to transfer even more decision-making responsibility to elite technocrats in government, the result will be to further exacerbate the discrepancy between knowledge and power that is at the root of the crisis.

Even before the latest lurch toward government expansion, the growing inequality of political power should have been cause for concern. Through both *scale creep* and *scope creep*, the power of politicians has increased dramatically. Scale creep means that a population increases while the size of the jurisdiction remains constant. Scope creep means that jurisdictions undertake more and more activities each year.

While political power has become more concentrated, information has become more diffuse. As knowledge expands, new specialties emerge. The incongruity between centralized government and decentralized knowledge becomes greater. Government institutions remain centralized and inflexible in sharp contrast with the Internet, which is decentralized, fluid, and therefore in close alignment with the information age.

How can we reverse the trend toward greater concentration of political power? A number of institutional reforms are available. They include substituting vouchers for direct government provision of public services; allowing citizens to flexibly create their own organizations to provide public goods; and allowing citizens to directly allocate funds for public goods, rather than delegate this power to representatives.

When I first began developing this book, I intended to use my local jurisdiction, Montgomery County of Maryland, as an illustration of concentrated power. I was struck by the fact that nine little-known County Council members can allocate a budget of $4.5 billion per year.

In September and October of 2008, however, an even larger example of concentrated power emerged. Treasury Secretary Henry Paulson asked for unprecedented authority to spend $700 billion to rescue the financial system from a crisis involving mortgage-backed securities. This impelled me to reshape this book.

As it happens, I spent a formative stage of my career, in the late 1980s and early 1990s, working for Freddie Mac, one of the major players in the mortgage securitization drama. Accordingly, I believe that I have a useful perspective to offer on the crisis. More importantly, I think that the crisis illustrates the main theme of this book. The financial meltdown and the ineffectual response dramatically show what can result from the discrepancy between the increased dispersion of knowledge and the increased concentration of power. Those who have the most knowledge about mortgage credit risk lack executive power, both in business and in government. Those who have the most power have inadequate knowledge.

This book has three main parts. Part one looks at the history of mortgage securitization, informed by my professional experience, on mortgage credit risk. To many pundits, securitization represents a form of Wall Street genius that ran amok, along the lines of a chemistry experiment that got out of control and caused an explosion. It is common to blame deregulation, suggesting something like a teenage party that lacked adult supervision and degenerated into debauchery and mayhem.

Instead, I will suggest that the financial crisis was the outcome of industrial policy, American-style, which promoted and protected the businesses that are tied to home-building, real estate selling, and mortgage indebtedness. In particular, this industrial policy made the financial system vulnerable to the discrepancy between dispersed knowledge and concentrated power.

This industrial policy was driven by business and government leaders who "knew" things that turned out not to be true. Wall Street executives believed that they possessed superior mathematical tools to manage risk. Banking regulators believed that risk-based capital regulations ensured a sound banking system. Politicians believed that home ownership rates can never be too high. Securities rating agencies believed that home prices can never fall nationally. Executives at companies like AIG insurance, Freddie Mac, and Fannie Mae believed that they were earning insurance premiums for taking minimal risk, so that they did not need to set aside much in the way of loss reserves or capital. In each case, there were people who knew otherwise, but those with the knowledge were not in positions of power to make decisions.

The second part of the book contrasts the trends in knowledge and power. Knowledge is becoming increasingly specialized. New species of jobs, products, and areas of expertise are appearing at an exponentially increasing rate. The knowledge at the center is shrinking relative to knowledge at the periphery. However, political power is moving in the opposite direction, with power at the center rising relative to power at the periphery. This discrepancy between knowledge and power has the potential to produce tension or conflict.

The third part of the book argues that democratic means have failed as a check on concentrated power. Instead, I advocate competitive government, in which citizens are empowered by the market mechanisms of choice and competition rather than the democratic mechanism of voice. I do not advocate any single comprehensive reform or constitutional change. Instead, I spell out a variety of institutional alternatives for providing public goods in a more decentralized manner.

Chapter 1
The Financial Crisis of 2008

I begin the discussion of the discrepancy between knowledge and power by reviewing the financial crisis of 2008. In looking at the history of the crisis, one can discern a pattern in which executives and regulators failed to comprehend the risks that were accumulating inside firms and within the system as a whole.

In a compelling fictional narrative, there are villains, victims, and heroes. A compelling account of the financial crisis of 2008 containing such characters can be given, but it would be fictional. A true villain has to know what he is doing. In the case of the financial crisis, key executives and heads of regulatory agencies were ignorant of what was happening until it was too late.

The primary candidates for the role of villain—the executives of banks, Wall Street firms, and insurance companies—did too poorly in the end to suggest willfulness. If these companies had done nothing but deliberately foist risks on others, they themselves would have survived. The fact that Bear Stearns, Lehman Brothers, and other companies took such large losses is indicative of self-deception.

My narrative of the crisis emphasizes a widespread gap between what people thought they knew and what was actually true. Executives had too much confidence in their risk management strategies. Regulators, too, had excessive confidence in the measures that they had in place to ensure safety and soundness of banks and other regulated institutions. The crisis was both a market failure and a government failure.

I will argue that some of the most important financial instruments implicated in the crisis, including mortgage-backed securities and credit default swaps, owed their existence to regulatory anomalies. In the way that they specified capital requirements, regulators gave their implicit blessing to risky mortgages laundered through securitization and to treating a broad portfolio of risky assets as if it were a safe asset.

The financial structure rested on a housing bubble. One question is whether there are natural forces that always make an economy prone to booms and busts. If so, then had the boom and bust not occurred in housing and mortgage lending, it would have taken place elsewhere. Perhaps the very ability of the economy to survive earlier financial debacles, such as the stock market crash of 1987 or the dotcom boom that collapsed in 2000, reinforced complacency on the part of investors and policymakers. Leaving that aside, I will concentrate on how the boom and bust occurred where it did.

Housing Industrial Policy

Housing and mortgage debt are heavily influenced by public policy. It might even be fair to say that housing is to the United States what manufacturing exports were to Japan in the decades following the Second World War—a sector viewed by government as critical for the health of the economy. Like manufacturing exports in Japan, housing in the United States has been the focus of industrial policy, in which government and private firms worked together in an attempt to maintain continuous expansion. Increased home ownership and cheap, accessible mortgage finance were major policy goals, regardless of which political party held Congress or the Presidency.

This housing industrial policy can be traced back quite far. However, I will start in 1968, which was the year that mortgage securitization made its debut. In that year, Lyndon B. Johnson was an unpopular President fighting an unpopular war in Vietnam. Under the circumstances, having to ask Congress to increase the limit on the national debt always caused friction and embarrassment for the Administration. At the time, the national debt included the funds raised by government housing agencies. In 1968, the government found two ways to get this debt off its books.

The Federal National Mortgage Association, which had been created in 1938 to fill the void left by bank failures, functioned by purchasing home loans from independent originators known as mortgage bankers. Fannie Mae, as it was later called, acted like a giant national bank, financing mortgages from all over the country. At that time, it did not issue any mortgage securities. Instead, it funded its holdings by issuing bonds as an agency of the Federal government. To get Fannie Mae debt off its books, the government privatized Fannie Mae by selling shares to investors. The government may have retained an implicit promise not to allow Fannie Mae to fail, but this implicit promise appeared nowhere on the government's balance sheet.

Selling Fannie Mae still left the government issuing debt to finance mortgages under loan programs of the Federal Housing Administration (FHA) and the Veterans' Administration (VA). To take these mortgage loans off the books, the Johnson Administration created the Government National Mortgage Association (GNMA), which pooled loans insured by FHA/VA into securities and sold them to investors. This meant that the government no longer had to issue its own bonds to finance these mortgages. However, the government continued to guarantee that FHA/VA mortgages would not default.

Mortgage securitization has always had two major advantages. One is that it permits accounting gimmicks, such as moving mortgages off the government books and thereby lowering the official national debt. Similar accounting tricks have been at work in every major surge in securitization.

The other major advantage of securitization is that it allows less-regulated firms to act more nimbly than depository institutions. When the regulated banking sector has been unable to satisfy mortgage demand, securitization has, for better or worse, stepped in to fill the gap. While the depository institutions (banks and savings and loan associations) have been restrained more firmly by state regulators or agencies in Washington, issuers of mortgage securities have been able to provide funds. Still, if the regulatory playing field had always been level, it is unlikely that securitization would have emerged.

Indirect Lending and Agency Costs

To understand the problems inherent in securitization, imagine that you are a bank executive faced with two alternative routes for obtaining mortgage loans: a direct route and an indirect route. In the direct route, your loans are originated by your own staff. You establish standards, policies, and procedures for loan origination. You choose the markets in which you would like to originate loans, and you will probably focus on communities where you know the local economy. You hire and train personnel to follow internal guidelines. Your compensation policies incorporate incentives for them to accept or reject applicants according to company policy. Once a loan is made, if the borrower misses a payment, your staff follows company procedures for contacting the borrower and resolving the problem.

In the indirect route, loans are originated by persons unknown to you, following guidelines established by someone else. The loans may come from communities with which you are totally unfamiliar. The originators may very well be paid on commission, which they can only receive if they close a loan—never if they reject an applicant. If the loan gets into trouble, you will have no control over how the delinquency is handled.

In the absence of any external pressures or regulatory distortions, no sane bank executive would choose the indirect route over the direct route. In economic jargon, the "agency costs" of the indirect route are prohibitive. The originators of mortgages in the indirect route are operating under incentives that are contrary to the bank's interest. The misalignment of incentives between the bank and those acting as its agents in the indirect route will force banks to incur additional costs to monitor and review the work of the originators. Even with the most diligent efforts, the bank is likely to incur higher losses from defaults, as originators squeeze bad loans through the cracks of the bank's monitoring systems.

It is surprising, therefore, that as of 2008, nearly three-fourths of mortgage debt in the United States had been originated using the indirect method. To reach this point required a combination of Wall Street ingenuity and regulatory anomalies.

Some of the ingenuity involved finding an intermediary to bear the risk of mortgage loan defaults. For example, GNMA securities are guaranteed by the government, with the default risk on the mortgages ultimately borne by FHA. As we will see, the concept of guaranteed securities spread to other types of mortgages, although the quality of the guarantees became suspect during the crisis period in 2008. Without the guarantees—or the apparent guarantees—indirect lending would not have been possible. Even with guarantees, there was nothing cost-effective about indirect lending. The main cost advantages of securitization came from accounting and regulatory anomalies.

The Growth of Securitization

In 1970, there were many regulatory constraints hampering savings and loans (S&Ls, also known as thrifts), the dominant mortgage lenders at the time. Their deposit interest rates were limited by government-set ceilings, under what was known as Regulation Q. Because of ever-rising inflation, market interest rates were much higher than Reg Q ceilings, and the thrifts were soon to be starved for funds. Nimbler, less regulated competitors—money market funds—siphoned money away from retail deposits.

Thrifts in California were particularly frustrated by a shortage of funds. At the time, depository institutions could not operate across state lines, and the relatively abundant savings in the eastern United States could not reach the west.

To address the mismatch between savings in the east and mortgage demand in the west, Congress established Freddie Mac, with a goal of creating a national "secondary market" in mortgages. Freddie Mac was placed under the Federal Home Loan Bank Board, the agency that had oversight of the savings and loans. Unlike the thrifts themselves, Freddie Mac could move funds from one coast to the other. For example, Freddie Mac could bundle mortgage loans originated by a thrift in California into securities that Freddie Mac could sell to a thrift located in New York.

Freddie Mac was able to do what the thrifts themselves were not able to do because of regulation. Had Regulation Q not been in effect, California thrifts could have increased interest rates on deposits to attract sufficient funds to allow them to meet mortgage demand using the direct method of lending. Alternatively, if restrictions on interstate banking had been lifted, a multi-state holding company could have channeled excess savings from its banks in the east to be used for mortgage loans by its banks in the west without resorting to indirect mortgage origination.

To make the secondary mortgage market efficient, Freddie Mac guaranteed security-holders against mortgage defaults. If a mortgage in a Freddie Mac security stopped making payments, Freddie Mac stepped in, pulled the mortgage out of the pool, and paid investors the full principal due on that mortgage. At that point, Freddie Mac would attempt to recover as much as it could through the foreclosure process.

Freddie Mac's role as guarantor of the mortgages that it securitized required a large and intricate operation to monitor, manage, and price mortgage credit risk. I became part of that operation, joining Freddie Mac in December of 1986. I spent much of my first few years there helping to implement a mortgage pricing model developed by Chester Foster and Robert Van Order, two economists who joined Freddie Mac after working for the Department of Housing and Urban Development.[1] The pricing methodology employed simulations of a variety of paths for house prices, with default probabilities depending on the house price scenario as well as characteristics of the mortgages. For example, loans for investment properties or for cash-out refinances had higher default risk than loans for owner-occupied purchases. Loans with low down payments had higher default risk than loans with higher down payments.

[1] Chester Foster and Robert Van Order, "An option based model of mortgage default" *Housing Finance Review* 3, no. 4 (1984): 351-372.

Late in 1989, I shifted to a different position at Freddie Mac where I helped implement its quality control sample. Because loans were being originated by third parties, Freddie Mac operated a large division devoted to monitoring the performance of these loan sellers. The quality control process selected a sample of loans for re-underwriting by Freddie Mac staff. Re-underwriting was costly both to Freddie Mac and to originators, so the idea of the sample was to try to select a minimum number of loans for re-underwriting in such a way as to identify originators who were failing to properly screen loan applicants and property characteristics. This was just one of the processes that Freddie Mac needed in order to compensate for the misalignment of incentives that exists in securitized lending.

In the early 1990s, I studied ways to automate the underwriting of loans at Freddie Mac. We came to realize that credit scoring had a number of advantages over human underwriting. It was cheaper, and the statistical methodology behind the scoring system made fewer errors—it rejected fewer good borrowers while accepting fewer bad borrowers. Finally, from the standpoint of indirect lending, switching from human underwriting to credit scoring based on data held by the large credit reporting services helped to eliminate one of the potential sources of misrepresentation on the part of loan originators, because they no longer had control over credit underwriting. Ironically, the gains in efficiency that credit scoring produced also set the stage for private securitization, in which Wall Street firms were able to make inroads into the mortgage market and threaten the dominance of Freddie Mac and Fannie Mae.

The 1970s were not kind to the savings and loan industry. With inflation out of control, market interest rates steadily rose. Relaxation of Regulation Q interest rate ceilings proved to be a mixed blessing. Although it enabled thrifts to raise interest rates to stem the loss of deposits, it raised the cost of funds above the rates that they were earning on mortgage loans originated in prior years, when inflation and interest rates had been lower.

In the late 1970s, Lew Ranieri and Robert Dall, two executives at the bond-trading firm of Salomon Brothers, created a vision of a U.S.

mortgage market dominated by securitization, which would enable investment banks to participate in the largest credit market in the world. With the thrift industry on the ropes, their timing was good. However, it took a combination of luck and intentional lobbying to shape the playing field to fulfill their vision.

Starting in 1980, newly appointed Federal Reserve Chairman Paul Volcker decided to break the back of inflation with contractionary monetary policy. Interest rates soared into the double-digits, and many thrifts became insolvent. However, before they were shut down by their regulators, many thrifts made one last desperate effort to borrow money to stay in business.

The S&Ls wanted to use their mortgage assets to raise cash, but they did not want to sell those mortgage assets. Under accounting rules that prevailed at the time, the thrifts were allowed to record their mortgage assets as if they had not declined in value. In fact, in an environment where new mortgages were being originated with interest rates of 12 percent, an old mortgage that carried a six percent interest rate and a $100,000 outstanding balance was worth approximately $50,000. Selling such loans would mean recognizing the losses, which would expose the negative net worth of the institution, which in turn would force regulators to shut it down.

At the time, some academics were arguing that thrifts should have been shut down regardless. Their point was that under market-value accounting, they should have recognized the losses on their mortgage loans even if they held them. However, market-value accounting was novel and unpopular—only after the crisis had passed was market-value accounting widely adopted by banking regulators around the world.

In summary, without selling mortgage loans, the thrifts could not raise cash to operate. On the other hand, if they sold the loans, they would have to recognize losses on the assets. The thrifts appeared to be in a trap.

Wall Street proposed a solution. They created a new security program at Freddie Mac called Guarantor. Under this program, a thrift would exchange a package of its old mortgages to Freddie Mac for a security backed by those mortgages. The security could then be used as collateral by the thrift to borrow against. Freddie Mac earned a fee (as high as two percent) for engaging in this purely paper transaction. Wall Street firms earned fees finding institutional investors to lend to thrifts, with the securities as collateral. The losers, ultimately, were the taxpayers, since most of the thrifts eventually still went bankrupt, having been bled by the fees and having made further unsound investments. The S&Ls were undone by inflation and interest-rate risk (and previous regulatory constraints). Securitization would address interest-rate risk while setting the stage for a credit risk crisis just over two decades later.

The key to the Guarantor program was a regulatory accounting ruling—much sought after by all parties—that the exchange of mortgages for a security backed by those mortgages did not require the thrift to mark the value of the security down to market value. Even though the loans that the thrifts received from institutions were based on market values, rather than book values, the thrifts were allowed to keep the securities on their books at fictional book values. Without this peculiar accounting treatment, Guarantor would not have gotten off the ground. Instead, thanks to regulators' tolerance of an accounting fiction, Guarantor became a large program at Freddie Mac. Fannie Mae, seeing the profit opportunity, entered the mortgage security business with its own version of Guarantor called Swap.

Up to this point, Fannie Mae and Freddie Mac operated differently. Freddie Mac primarily bought loans from thrifts, packaged the mortgages into securities, and sold the securities to investors. Fannie Mae primarily bought loans from mortgage bankers and held them in its portfolio, financed by debt. Thus, Fannie Mae took interest rate risk as well as mortgage credit risk.

In 1988, Freddie Mac stock was divided among thrifts. In 1989, the stock was made available to the public on the New York Stock Exchange, thus privatizing the agency just as Fannie Mae had been privatized 20 years earlier. In its new form, Freddie Mac adopted and increasingly implemented Fannie Mae's strategy of buying loans for its portfolio, funded with debt.

Capital Requirements Advantage GSEs

By 2003, Freddie Mac and Fannie Mae together held 50 percent of the mortgage debt outstanding in the United States. Depository institutions could no longer compete effectively with the two companies, known as Government-Sponsored Enterprises, or GSEs.

The key competitive advantage of the GSEs involved capital requirements. Banks are required to hold eight percent capital against risk-weighted assets. In 1989, the United States adopted requirements developed by the Bank for International Settlements (BIS). These are known as the Basel I agreements, because the BIS is located in Basel, Switzerland. Under Basel I, mortgage loans have a risk weight of 50 percent, so that the capital requirement for a mortgage loan would be four percent. More refined capital requirements, known as Basel II, allow low-risk mortgages, with down payments of more than 40 percent, to receive a risk weight of 20 percent, while loans with down payments of 20 to 40 percent have a risk weight of 35 percent.

For mortgage loans with a down payment of 20 percent or more, bank capital requirements are much higher than they are for Freddie Mac and Fannie Mae. Freddie Mac and Fannie Mae are subject to different regulations. In practice, their ratio of capital to assets was less than three percent, which was well below that of banks.

The GSEs capital requirements were based in part on a stress test. They were supposed to hold sufficient capital to be able to withstand a decline of housing prices comparable to a severe historical recession. Whether this stress test was calculated properly for the portfolio of high-risk loans that the firms acquired starting in around 2004 is questionable. However, for loans with substantial down payments made to credit-worthy borrowers, the capital requirements for the GSEs were more accurate than the crude requirements given to banks.

As of 2003, the capital requirements were an anomaly that artificially restrained depository institutions from competing effectively with the GSEs. However, capital requirements were not yet a source of instability in the banking system. Problems in the banking system developed only when securitized sub-prime mortgage lending took off.

Private Securitization

B y 2004, a number of market developments caused the emergence of a significant segment of mortgage loans with low down payments, originated by mortgage brokers and securitized by Wall Street firms. These mortgage securities are called private securities, to distinguish them from securities issued by the GSEs.

Private securitization reached for a segment of the market that was considered too high-risk by the GSEs. That segment included borrowers with impaired credit or with income levels that historically would have been considered too low to qualify for the housing expenses being incurred. This so-called sub-prime market was dominated by private securitization.

One of the developments that promoted private securitization was credit scoring. In the late 1990s, credit scoring had replaced human underwriting at the GSEs. In addition to being inexpensive and reasonably accurate, credit scoring helped to reduce the agency costs associated with indirect lending. A credit score is objectively calculated by an independent specialty firm (Fair Isaac is the most well known), which takes away the concern that a third-party underwriter could be hiding flaws in the borrower's credit history.

Another development was the concept of risk tranches. The cash flows from a pool of mortgages could be divided in such a way that all of the first, say five percent, of mortgage defaults would be borne by the subordinate security, with senior securities insulated from that portion of default risk. Insulated in this way, senior securities were able to earn AA or AAA ratings from agencies, which in turn made those securities eligible to be held in institutional portfolios. For example, a bank could hold a AA security and have it receive a 20 percent risk weight.

In reality, a senior security backed by sub-prime mortgages with down payments of less than five percent was much more likely to suffer losses than a prime mortgage with a 20 percent down payment made by the bank. But even under Basel II, capital regulations gave a 20 percent risk weight to the security and a 35 percent risk weight to the safe mortgage loan. The regulators were telling the banks to prefer

securities backed by someone else's junk loans over safe loans originated directly by the bank.

The AAA and AA ratings of mortgage securities came under fire
once Congress and the press began to investigate the causes of the crisis in the fall of 2008. Relative to those ratings, the actual performance
of the securities has been dismal, and a Congressional hearing in October uncovered internal memos in the agencies warning that the ratings were inaccurate. The problems with the ratings are discussed
extensively in a paper by Joshua D. Coval, Jakob W. Jurek, and Erik
Stafford.[2] They cite evidence that at least one of the rating agencies,
Fitch, did not even consider the possibility of house price declines
when it rated mortgage securities.

Economists report that large Wall Street firms had internal models of mortgage default risk that showed that a AAA-rated mortgage
security was far riskier than a AAA-rated corporate bond. These risk
models were used by sophisticated investors, such as hedge funds, to
value mortgage-backed securities. On the other hand, the ratings
made a difference to less-sophisticated investors, particularly banks,
given the incentives created for the latter by capital requirements.[3] I
should note that the rating agency structure was fixed by SEC regulations in 1975, effectively making new entry into the rating agency
market impossible.

Innovation Feeds a Bubble

The financial innovations of credit scoring, senior-subordinated
private mortgage securities, and loans with low down payments
served to broaden the mortgage market. As more households became
able to borrow, the demand for homes expanded and prices rose. This
had the effect of reducing mortgage defaults. A homeowner's equity

---

[2] Joshua D. Coval, Jakub W. Jurek, and Erik Stafford, "The Economics of Structured Finance" *Harvard Business School Finance* Working Paper No. 09-060 (2008).
http://papers.ssrn.com/sol3/papers.cfm?abstract_id=1287363

[3] See the September 15, 2008 press briefing of the Shadow Financial Regulatory Committee. http://www.aei.org/events/eventID.1790/event_detail.asp

consists of the down payment plus any price appreciation that has taken place since the home was purchased. When that equity is positive, a borrower who finds it difficult to make the payments on a home will either sell the house or refinance it with a larger mortgage rather than default.

As long as house prices were appreciating, the performance of mortgage securities was excellent. This encouraged more lending, which encouraged more home ownership, which in turn fed into faster house price appreciation. Much of the new home buying was speculative. Over 15 percent of home loans in 2005 and 2006 went for non-owner occupants, meaning that they were bought for investment purposes. This was more than triple the rate of investor loans that were made a decade earlier. Economist William Wheaton estimates that the housing stock grew by six percentage points more than the number of households, as the speculative demand for housing boosted production.

Policymakers encouraged this burst of housing speculation. Enforcement of the Community Reinvestment Act for banks and the "affordable housing goals" for the GSEs meant that these companies had to make sure that a sizable percentage of mortgage loans went to low-income borrowers, even as the run-up in house prices was increasing the ratio of median home prices to median incomes. While traditional rules of thumb suggested that a house price should be no more than three times the borrower's income, in some California counties the ratio of price to income approached ten.

Pressed to meet their "affordable housing" goals, the GSEs for the first time began to back sub-prime loans and other mortgages with low down payments. Despite internal warnings that these purchases threatened the safety and soundness of Freddie Mac and Fannie Mae, the two companies took on unprecedented exposure to credit risk. Under the stress test methodology, the mortgages that the GSEs were now guaranteeing would have required much higher levels of capital than traditional mortgage loans. However, concerned with not diluting earnings, the companies postponed raising the capital needed to restore compliance with the stress tests.

Suits vs. Geeks

The conflict between executive decisions and internal warnings at Freddie Mac and Fannie Mae was an example of what I call the "suits vs. geeks" divide. The geeks were staff who used statistical models to predict mortgage defaults under alternative scenarios and to translate those simulations into values of various mortgage securities. The suits were executives with decision-making authority. Often, the geeks saw lower values and higher risk in the securities than the suits, but the suits were in charge of setting corporate portfolio policy.

Innovative financial instruments, such as senior-subordinated structures for private mortgage securities, were understood by financial engineers (the geeks). They were understood less well by executives and major policymakers (the suits). The geeks regarded the AA and AAA designations by the rating agencies as faulty. The suits took the ratings as reliable.

Geeks watched suits develop ever-increasing confidence in quantitative risk management, including credit scoring and bond default modeling. The latter was used to create the market for credit default swaps, which I discuss below. Once their initial skepticism was overcome, suits became excessively confident in quantitative risk modeling. They confused the favorable context of rising home prices with a fundamental reduction in risk.

The geeks treated mortgage securities as having embedded put options that were very close to being in the money. That is, the security-holder has effectively sold mortgage borrowers an option to default. Borrowers are more likely to exercise that option if their equity in the home is negative, in which case the option is in the money. When initial down payments are low, it only takes a small decline in home prices to make the default option in the money, which would be exercised particularly aggressively by non-owner-occupied property investors (recall that the rate of investor loans had tripled by 2005 and 2006 to over 15 percent of all mortgages).

The suits treated mortgage securities as bonds, ignoring the power of the embedded options. In August and September, when policymakers began to perceive the severity of the crisis, the suits thought that mortgage securities could not possibly have lost as much value as their market prices indicated. Federal Reserve Board Chairman Ben Bernanke insisted that if the securities were "held to maturity" that they would have higher values. Treasury Secretary Henry Paulson proposed to have the government buy and hold these securities in order to "unclog" the financial system. However, this thesis, which in effect was arguing that the geeks had mispriced mortgage securities, proved to be incorrect. The banks that had invested heavily in these securities were truly under-capitalized. The mistakes had been made by the suits, not the geeks.

The differences between management and staff may not be unique to the financial industry. In his personal observations on the investigation of the disaster of the Space Shuttle Challenger, physicist Richard Feynman wrote, "Why do we find such an enormous disparity between the management estimate and the judgment of the engineers? It would appear that, for whatever purpose, be it for internal or external consumption, the management of NASA exaggerates the reliability of its product, to the point of fantasy."[4]

In large corporations and government agencies, the people who get ahead are those with confidence in themselves, faith in the soundness of the organization, and trust in the judgment of leaders. Doubters and skeptics are derailed for being poor team players with a negative attitude. Leaders of large organizations often are hostile to new ideas. However, once embraced, innovation can come to be regarded too highly. In the case of credit scoring, securitization, and credit default swaps, executives and regulators attributed more power and reliability to the innovations than was actually warranted.

There is a phenomenon in social psychology known as the "fundamental attribution error." Experiments have shown that people underestimate the role of context in determining behavior. The classic experiment has the subject watch an actor read a speech.

[4] R.P. Feynman, "Personal Observations on the Reliability of the Shuttle" http://www.fotuva.org/feynman/challenger-appendix.html

The subject knows that the actor did not write the speech, but nonetheless the subject tends to attribute to the actor the beliefs in the speech.

In retrospect, the apparent success of many of the mortgage practices that developed in recent years was due to the context of rising home prices. However, key executives and regulators instead committed the fundamental attribution error. They took the view that skillful innovation was the major reason for the success of securitization. Only when the context changed did this error become apparent.

A Complex Phenomenon

Overall, I would describe the housing and mortgage credit bubble as a complex phenomenon that emerged for a number of reasons. I would assign much of the blame to the growth of securitization, which in turn was affected by a number of regulatory anomalies, notably capital requirements that favored securities backed by risky mortgages over ordinary direct mortgage lending, even when the latter included loans with sizable down payments.

I would assign another large share of the blame to the emergence of a large volume of mortgage loans with low down payments. This created a situation in which housing equity consisted largely of price appreciation. That accentuated the housing cycle, because with no money down almost everyone can buy a home when prices are rising and almost no one can buy a home when prices stop rising.

Finally, I would assign some blame to the "suits vs. geeks" divide. Knowledge of mortgage credit risk and the behavior of mortgage securities was separated from power over portfolio decisions. The executives who took on mortgage credit risk at banks, insurance companies, and the GSEs did not fully appreciate the chances they were taking. The financial engineers who were responsible for the creation and pricing of complex mortgage securities did not educate key executives or heads of regulatory agencies about the true nature of the new products. It was easier to believe that securitization reflected the "genius" of Wall Street rather than a dubious process artificially stimulated by regulatory anomalies.

William Wheaton and Gleb Nechayev described the nature of the housing bubble and the role played by securitization in a paper written in May 2006 when the boom was at its peak:[5]

- In 1996, sub-prime loans amounted to less than $100 billion and less than 12 percent of mortgage originations. In 2005, sub-prime mortgages amounted to over $600 billion and accounted for over 26 percent of all mortgage originations.
- Adjusted for inflation, from 1996 to 2005, house prices rose 55 percent, while average per capita income rose only 17 percent. However, a drop in mortgage interest rates served to offset the rise in home prices, leaving monthly mortgage payments in line with income.
- From 1996 to 2005, median rents rose 10 percent while median prices rose 45 percent.
- "Between 1965 and 1995 the home ownership rate bounced around between 63 and 64 percent. Since 1995 it has jumped five percentage points and is now near 70%."

They also point out that in the last few years of the boom, housing production exceeded new household formation by 30–50 percent. Moreover, investor loans rose to more than 15 percent of the total.

In sum, housing demand was expanded by speculation and by the availability of mortgage credit, particularly for sub-prime borrowers. This caused prices and construction to rise above sustainable levels. Then came a crash, where these forces went into reverse.

One problem with this particular view of the story is that only 10 percent of subprime loans went to first-time homebuyers. However, given that sub-prime lending grew to 20 percent of mortgage originations, this channel still delivered a considerable segment of first-

[5] William C. Wheaton and Gleb Nechayev, "Past Housing 'Cycles' and the Current Housing 'Boom': What's Different this Time?" (2006) http://web.mit.edu/cre/students/faculty/pdf/HousingBubble.pdf

time home buyers. Moreover, the availability of the refinancing channel also served to encourage home buying and speculation. In fact, 55
percent of sub-prime loans were refinances.[6]

Other Narratives

A number of other factors that other narratives treat as important
are, in my view, less critical. For example, many pundits wish to
blame the "general atmosphere of deregulation" and "free-market ideology." However, few specific policies are cited in this narrative. The
fact is that securitization, house price inflation, and the lack of under-
standing of risk-taking on the part of executives were little influenced
by specific relaxation of financial regulation. In my view, the most
powerful regulatory impetus—the anomaly in risk-based capital standards—was subtle and cannot be attributed to any particular regulatory
ideology.

Another way to look at the narrative of deregulation as the cause
of the crisis is to compare the sorts of regulations that were being proposed with what would have served to prevent the crisis. For example,
some policy analysts wanted to stop the practice of "yield-spread premiums," in which a mortgage broker could earn a larger commission
for charging a borrower a higher interest rate than circumstances warranted. Ending this practice perhaps would have lowered interest rates
for some borrowers, but it might not have reduced the expansion of
lending, which is what fed the housing bubble.

Similarly, economist Edward Gramlich and others proposed having Freddie Mac and Fannie Mae become more involved in the sub-
prime mortgage market to improve lending standards and better
regulate mortgage originators. Again, this might have curbed abuses,
but it would not have curtailed overall lending.

There were calls to "rein in" Freddie Mac and Fannie Mae. However, on close examination, the concern was with interest rate risk and
the size of the retained portfolios. The critics were not suggesting that

---

[6] Michael Calhoun, Center for Responsible Lending, "The Future of Subprime Mortgages" (2007). http://www.urban.org/Pressroom/otherevents/subprimemortgages.cfm

Freddie and Fannie guarantee fewer mortgages and create fewer securities. The criticism instead was focused on the volume of securities that Freddie and Fannie held in their own portfolios, financed by issuing risky debt.

Holding mortgages in a portfolio requires a corporation to finance those mortgages. This is a challenge because mortgages have variable duration, depending on borrowers' prepayment behavior. To manage their interest rate risk, Freddie Mac and Fannie Mae developed large, complex balance sheets. Critics feared that either mistakes or unexpected market volatility could impose losses at the GSEs in excess of their capital.

In fact, complex balance sheets and interest rate risk did not turn out to be the locus of the problem at the GSEs. Instead, they incurred large losses in the much simpler business of providing guarantees against mortgage default.

Freddie and Fannie could have satisfied most of their critics while increasing their volume of mortgage guarantees by retaining fewer securities in portfolios and instead selling more securities to investors. However, this would not have reduced their exposure to mortgage credit risk.

The key to stopping the bubble would have been to reduce securitization and lower the demand for housing. For example, bank regulators could have scrutinized the risk of mortgage securities more carefully and assigned higher risk weights for regulatory capital. With respect to Freddie Mac and Fannie Mae, OFHEO, which regulated the GSEs, could have enforced stricter capital requirements, particularly for high risk loans.

Regulators could have taken more steps to discourage speculation. Higher risk weights could have been assigned to mortgage loans for speculative purposes (non-owner-occupied loans) and for securities backed by such loans. Regulators could have required banks and the GSEs to control their exposure in regions where there had been unusually high levels of house price appreciation.

None of these regulations was ever under consideration. The necessary regulations were not standard regulations that were suddenly dropped. They would have represented entirely new regulatory initiatives, and they would have been met with skepticism and derision by members of Congress and the Administration who were pleased with the rising trend of home ownership and household wealth. We know in hindsight what the right regulations would have been. However, such regulations were not plausible at the time. That is the problem with the deregulation narrative. There is a complete disconnect between the regulatory changes that were made or that were proposed at the time and those that would have prevented the crisis.

Another narrative is that the Community Reinvestment Act and the promotion of lending to racial minorities and borrowers with bad credit histories was a critical factor. However, I believe that it was the nature of the mortgage loans—in particular, the relaxation of requirements for making a significant down payment—that caused the housing cycle to get out of control. The problem with the loans made from 2003–2007 was not the color of the borrowers' skins or the content of their credit reports. It was the fact that public policy so heavily favored mortgage indebtedness, and hence housing speculation, rather than true home ownership. Had the subsidies and mandates instead been geared toward encouraging new homebuyers to save for down payments, the impact would have been less destabilizing and better for all concerned.

One point to bear in mind is that about half of all mortgage loans that went to minorities in 2006 were sub-prime loans. Therefore, regulatory targets for Freddie Mac and Fannie Mae in minority lending might very well have forced the GSEs to enter the sub-prime market. Moreover, a number of policy experts, including the late Edward Gramlich, who was an early opponent of unregulated sub-prime lending, were happy to see the GSEs involved in that market. Their hope was that the GSEs would bring a degree of standardization and "adult supervision" to the market.[7]

Another narrative is that Alan Greenspan kept interest rates too low from 2001 through 2003. However, the overwhelming consensus

---

[7] See the Urban Institute's forum, "The Future of Subprime Mortgages," held on July 25, 2007. http://www.urban.org/Pressroom/otherevents/subprimemortgages.cfm

of economic theory at the time was that monetary policy should be used to stabilize inflation, not to pop bubbles. Moreover, much of the run-up in house prices took place after Greenspan's term as Fed Chairman ended. Ben Bernanke succeeded Greenspan in 2006. Currently, Bernanke is much more admired than Greenspan in academia and in the press. There seems to be a tendency to exaggerate the blame placed on Greenspan and to minimize the problems attributed to Bernanke. (Bernanke was also a member of the Board of Governors of the Federal Reserve System from 2002 through 2004.)

Credit Default Swaps

Still another narrative is that new derivative instruments made the system fragile because of counterparty risk. Credit default swaps are often cited as an example of a market that might have been better regulated by an exchange. With a credit default swap, the buyer of a swap pays a regular fee equal to a percent of the bond's principal value. The seller of a swap agrees that in the event of a default, the seller will purchase the bond from the swap buyer for its full principal amount. Thus, the credit default swap acts like an insurance policy on the bond.

Credit default swaps were traded privately, with investment banks acting as brokers. That meant that there was counterparty risk. Counterparty risk is when one party to a contract could default on that contract. In particular, the buyer of a credit default swap has to worry about whether the seller will truly make good in the event that the bond default occurs.

As the credit default swap market grew, some policy experts recommended that swaps should be traded on an organized exchange. Exchanges, such as the Chicago Mercantile Exchange (where commodity contracts are traded) or the New York Stock Exchange (where stocks are traded) eliminate counterparty risk. For example, suppose that we are talking about corn for delivery in three months. A large food processor might contract with a specific farmer in March to deliver corn in August. That would involve counterparty risk, where either the farmer or the food processor might default in August.

Instead, the food processor might buy corn futures on an organized exchange. Meanwhile, the farmer might sell corn futures on the exchange. The farmer and the food processor are no longer counterparties to one another. Instead, each is making a separate transaction with the exchange. If the farmer defaults, it is the exchange that bears the cost, not the food processor. It is up to the exchange to set up margin requirements, capital requirements, and eligibility rules to protect itself from defaults.

In my opinion, the problem with credit default swaps is not counterparty risk. The problem is that there is no natural seller of default swaps. With corn futures, there is a natural buyer (the food processor) and a natural seller (the farmer). With credit default swaps, there is a natural buyer (the holder of a risky corporate bond), but there is no natural seller. Without a natural seller, I doubt that an organized exchange can work.

In practice, the sellers of credit default swaps are relying on two strategies, neither of which is really sound. One strategy is diversification. That means that a large seller, such as an insurance company, will have many swaps outstanding, but only a few defaults will occur at a time. The analogy would be with a large life insurance company, which can presume that only a small fraction of policyholders will die at any one time. However, the crisis of 2008 made a mockery of diversification as the threat of defaults became widespread.

Once again, capital requirements give rise to an anomaly. One way to think about credit default swaps is that some quantitative financial engineers believe that a diversified portfolio of B-rated bonds can have lower risk and a higher reward than a lone AA bond. However, this diversification is not recognized by bank capital regulations. If the financial engineers are correct, then there is a profit opportunity for a AAA-rated insurance company to insure B-rated bonds held by banks, allowing banks to sneak B-rated bonds past regulators and allowing the insurance company to benefit from the diversification strategy.

The anomaly is that bank capital requirements make no allowance for gains from diversification, while they accept the insurance company's guarantee as legitimate. This is inconsistent. Either a portfolio of B-rated bonds truly can have lower risk than a lone AA bond, in which case bank capital requirements should say so; or else the claim is false that a portfolio of B-rated bonds has low risk because of diversification (the risks may in fact be highly correlated), in which case the capital requirements should recognize that under adverse circumstances the insurance company that sells the credit default swap may not be able to fulfill its obligation, which means that banks should not be able to lower the capital required to hold B-rated bonds by purchasing credit default swaps. In other words, with consistent capital regulations, diversification either does or does not substantially reduce the risk of low-rated bonds. If it does, then banks can undertake the diversification themselves. If it does not, then having an insurance company undertake the diversification does not reduce the risk to banks of holding those bonds.

Apart from diversification, another strategy for selling credit default swaps is dynamic hedging. Suppose that the seller of a default swap on a bond issued by XYZ Corporation starts to suspect that the probability of a default on that bond is increasing. The seller can hedge its risk by selling short either XYZ Corporation stock or other XYZ Corporation bonds. In the event of a default, the loss that the seller will take by having to purchase the defaulted bond at par will be offset by the gains on the short-selling.

The problem with dynamic hedging is that it only works in a relatively stable market, in which few others are attempting similar strategies. When everyone is trying dynamic hedging at once, the result is a wave of short-selling that overwhelms markets.

Overall, then, if dynamic hedging is used by sellers of credit default swaps, they generate systemic risk. The individual swap sellers form contingency plans, which, in the aggregate, are not compatible. When swap sellers perceive an increase in risk, they all seek to short securities simultaneously, creating the equivalent of a bank run. This run would occur just as easily if swaps were traded on an exchange as if they were traded over-the-counter.

Another aspect of credit default swaps is that they are subject to liquidity risk, even if the fundamental calculations of default risk are correct. Credit default swaps are like options that start out deeply out of the money. Initially, the probability of default might be thought to be much less than one percent. The seller of the swap is thus collecting a fee for selling a put option that is very unlikely to be exercised.

Because the put option is so far out of the money, its value can change even if it remains well out of the money. That is, if the probability of default goes from one in ten thousand to one in one hundred, the value of the swap goes way up (meaning that the seller's net worth goes way down), even though there is still a low likelihood that the seller will have to take a loss. This can cause the sellers of credit default swaps to suffer liquidity and solvency problems even if none of the bonds actually defaults!

A story in the *Wall Street Journal* of October 31, 2008 explains how this affected AIG insurance, a major seller of credit default swaps:

> The buyers of the swaps—AIG's "counterparties" or trading partners on the deals—typically have the right to demand collateral from AIG if the securities being insured by the swaps decline in value, or if AIG's own corporate-debt rating is cut… The credit crisis hammered the markets for debt securities, sparking tough negotiations between AIG and its trading partners over how much more collateral AIG should have to post."[8]

Suppose that an insurer has sold a credit default swap on bond X. When the probability of a bond X default is really low, the option embedded in the credit default swap is far out of the money. Neither party has to be concerned that the option will be exercised. However, once the probability of default rises to some level of plausibility, say five percent, the seller of the swap is going to have to demonstrate the ability to make good on the swap. In an organized exchange, the seller would have to meet a margin call. In the over-the-counter market, the seller is forced to post collateral, which acts like a margin call. Even when default is still unlikely and the option is still out of the money, the margin calls can strain the balance sheet of the seller of the swap.

[8] "Behind AIG's Fall, Risk Models Failed to Pass Real-World Test," *Wall Street Journal Online*, October 31, 2008. http://online.wsj.com/article/SB122538449722784635.html

In addition, as the probability of a default on bond X rises, the value of the default swap changes adversely for the seller of the swap. This means that the insurer must recognize a loss, even though default remains unlikely.

Thus, even without a single default, an increase in the likelihood of defaults can undermine the seller of default swaps. The seller may lose liquidity due to margin calls or lose solvency due to the change in the value of the swaps.

A useful analogy might be with a company that sells flood insurance in areas along the Gulf Coast. On average, the insurance policies are profitable. If it wanted to, the insurance company could sell its book of business to competitors and receive cash in compensation. However, if it tried to unload its book of business at a time when there is a hurricane threatening to make landfall, it would not receive cash. Instead, it would have to pay another insurance company to take on that risk. The chances may still be high that the insurance policies will be profitable—the hurricane may dissipate or perhaps make landfall in a relatively unpopulated area. As of 2008, the sellers of credit default swaps on mortgage securities were in the potential path of a hurricane. Their positions might have been tenable, but nobody else would have wanted to trade places with AIG or other credit default swap sellers.

There are many ways for financial institutions to get caught up in processes that amount to selling put options that are far out of the money. The GSEs, by providing guarantees of mortgages, were selling put options that were out of the money as long as house prices were not falling sharply. Holders of senior tranches in mortgage securities were in the same position. A lesson of this crisis is that sellers of out-of-the-money options can become too complacent about the risks that are being taken to earn the option premium. As the probability increases that the options will be exercised, the seller's institutional viability can be undermined long before the options actually are in the money.

A deeper narrative of the financial crisis is that risk-taking tends to be cyclical, and that the housing bubble reflected a boom in risk-taking. In the period when the bubble was inflating, Federal Reserve Chairman Ben Bernanke himself spoke of the "global savings glut" that was helping to feed U.S. credit markets. Rapidly growing economies, particularly in Asia, produced incomes that grew faster than consumption. Having experienced currency crises in the 1990s, Asian investors, including central governments, sought dollar-denominated investments. This large increase in savings found its way into the U.S. housing market. As I noted earlier, one could argue that if housing finance had been better regulated, the global savings glut would simply have found its way into another risky arena, leading to a different bubble and a different locus for the crisis. There might have been a bubble in genetic therapy development or "green" energy or robotics or nanotechnology, with projects enthusiastically funded that ultimately failed to produce economically useful outcomes. If such a bubble or bubbles could have exceeded the dotcom bubble in intensity and international scope, it might have produced a crisis of the magnitude we observed when the housing bubble collapsed.

Crisis was not Predicted

Although some prognosticators saw elements of the crisis as it was forming, no one predicted the exact nature of the crisis. If there were a number of economists who saw the house price bubble as a boulder poised to fall, almost no one predicted the financial avalanche that ensued. The full web of connections between securitization, weakening of loan standards, the house price bubble, and systemic financial risk were not seen until it was too late.

For example, the Shadow Financial Regulatory Committee and other critics of the GSEs issued many warnings about a potential meltdown at Freddie Mac or Fannie Mae. However, most of their concern was with interest rate risk rather than with credit risk. That is, if Freddie Mac and Fannie Mae had only guaranteed mortgages but not held them in portfolio, much of the fears of the critics would have been alleviated.

Other experts questioned the growth of derivatives. These are financial contracts that reallocate the risks that are inherent in certain securities. For example, if you hold a corporate bond, you face the risk that the corporation will not be able to make its payments. By purchasing a credit default swap, you can transfer that risk to the seller of the swap.

In theory, derivatives reallocate risk to parties that are better able to bear that risk. In practice, many derivatives have been used successfully for years. However, in retrospect, I think that credit default swaps were sold by too many parties that did not have adequate plans or reserves for backing those swaps. That was the problem with AIG insurance, for example. Still, I think few people predicted the way that credit swaps would destabilize the financial system by causing short-selling of the securities of weak firms. Many critics continue to believe instead that the only problem with credit default swaps is that they were not traded on an organized exchange.

A number of economists perceived that house prices rose faster than inflation starting in the late 1990s. Still, it was not completely clear that the level of house prices was unsustainable. Because of low mortgage rates, the monthly payments had not risen substantially. In 2004, I took the view that the bubble was in interest rates. That is, I thought that interest rates were too low relative to long-term inflation trends. The implication was that there might be a slowdown in house price appreciation, but only because of higher interest rates. In fact, interest rates increased a bit, but the rise in home prices accelerated.

Indeed, as with any bubble, early diagnoses lost credibility. If a commentator said in 2003 or 2004 that house prices were too high, events of the next few years appeared to prove that commentator wrong. Successful forecasting of prices in a bubble requires more than just recognizing a bubble. In addition, one has to predict when the point will be reached where the bubble can no longer inflate. Instead, those who warn too early tend to have their warnings forgotten until well after the bubble has popped.

Even those who saw a bubble tended to foresee limited impact of a crash. For example, Paul Krugman was concerned that housing construction was carrying the economy. In a memorable column in 2005, Krugman wrote,

> On one side, domestic spending is swollen by the housing bub-
> ble, which has led both to a huge surge in construction and to
> high consumer spending, as people extract equity from their
> homes. On the other side, we have a huge trade deficit, which
> we cover by selling bonds to foreigners. As I like to say, these
> days Americans make a living by selling each other houses, paid
> for with money borrowed from China.[9]

Krugman and other macroeconomists worried about a housing bubble thought that the big problem with a crash would be the need to re-orient the American economy away from consumer spending and housing construction. Instead, the industries that would need to expand would be those that engage in exports or compete with imports. The concern they had was that a sudden withdrawal of foreign savings would force these adjustments to take place too quickly.

Indeed, there were several economists worried about house prices. In addition to Krugman, Dean Baker, Edward Leamer, and Robert Shiller also issued warnings that prices were out of line with fundamentals. There were other economists worried about the size of the portfolios at Freddie Mac and Fannie Mae. There were still other observers who were uneasy about the growth of derivatives and the complexity of the interconnections in financial markets.

A fairly typical analysis that was written well before prices peaked was an article in *FDIC Outlook* in 2004 by FDIC senior economist Cynthia Angell:

> The history of U.S. home prices suggests a clear potential for
> home prices to decline in individual markets, particularly in
> cities that have shown wide price swings in the past and where
> prices recently have risen dramatically. However, this same his-
> tory also strongly suggests that it is highly unlikely that home
> prices will fall precipitously across the entire country.[10]

[9] Paul Krugman, "Greenspan and the Bubble," *New York Times*, August 29, 2005. http://www.nytimes.com/2005/08/29/opinion/29krugman.html?_r=1&oref=slogin

[10] Cynthia Angell, "Housing Bubble Concerns and the Outlook for Mortgage Credit Quality," *FDIC Outlook*, 2004. http://www.fdic.gov/bank/analytical/regional/ro20041q/na/infocus.html

Indeed, part of the conventional wisdom during the housing bubble was that a nationwide home price decline would be unprecedented. Actually, there was some validity to the view that regional variation would be more pronounced than any nationwide fall in prices. There were in fact a number of locations that were spared precipitous declines in 2007 and 2008, while other areas, particularly in California, suffered very large price drops.

Angell's article presciently highlighted the dangers of sub-prime lending and the increase in mortgages with low down payments. It warned,

> more than three-quarters of currently outstanding mortgage debt has been originated in the past three years, thanks primarily to robust home purchase and refinance activity facilitated by record low mortgage rates. With these loans underwritten on the basis of recent high collateral values, a decline in home values in some markets could lead to default activity and losses to residential lenders. In particular, high-risk borrowers may default in increasing numbers should interest rates rise and home prices fall.[11]

As it turned out, the mortgages that were originated from 2001 through 2003 continued to benefit from house price appreciation. However, the article was correct in implying that when a house price boom stalls, it will be the most recent mortgages and the riskiest of those mortgages that are at the greatest risk to default.

It is reasonable to suggest that many experienced financial industry executives and regulators shared at least a mild concern about home prices and changing trends in mortgage finance at this time. However, the period of 2004–2006 saw no significant regulatory moves to curtail lending to risky borrowers or in regions where house prices had risen far faster than incomes. If the private sector was becoming increasingly prone to making systematically bad decisions, regulators were just as unable or unwilling to apply brakes to the process.

What no one was able to do, apparently, was connect the dots. That is, no one foresaw that the end of the housing bubble would cas-

[11] Ibid.

cade through the financial system, leading to losses of wealth that far exceeded the change in the market value of homes. No one foresaw that beyond the fundamental wealth losses due to lower house prices, there would be liquidity crises at Fannie Mae, Freddie Mac, the large investment banks, and AIG insurance, as investors lost confidence in the capital adequacy of those companies. The equivalent of bank runs that took place at these institutions, as well as others around the world, magnified the effect of the housing crash far beyond $5 trillion or so that presumably was lost if the peak value of housing in the United States was about $22 billion and prices fell by 20 to 25 percent.

As of late 2007, the financial crisis was referred to as the "sub-prime crisis." It appeared that the brunt of the problem was going to be borne by mortgage borrowers and by the unregulated segment of the mortgage origination market that had emerged over the preceding four years. There was no mention of vulnerability in the regulated sector, including banks and the GSEs.[12]

Even when it was clear that house prices were no longer rising and that home ownership was no longer going to expand, no one foresaw the vulnerability of regulated financial institutions to sub-prime investments. Only when it was far too late did the full extent of the damage become known.

During the upswing, some observers thought that the expansion of home ownership and the sub-prime market represented progress, as minorities and other disadvantaged groups gained more access to credit markets. Many observers thought that securitization was a superior form of mortgage production. Hardly anyone took notice of the large share of loans going to investors rather than owner-occupants, which we have seen reached more than 15 percent in 2005 and 2006. Apart from some obscure academic papers, no one seems to have taken note of the way that capital regulations artificially favored securitization over direct lending.

---

[12] For example, see: Alan Blinder, "Six Fingers of Blame in the Mortgage Mess," *New York Times*, September 30, 2007. http://www.nytimes.com/2007/09/30/business/30view.html

The Response to the Crisis

The government's response to the crisis was to seize unprecedented power. The first unprecedented move was for the Federal Reserve to assume some of the liabilities of an investment bank: Bear Stearns. Prior to this, investment banks had been considered outside the Fed's jurisdiction, which consists of commercial banks. Commercial banks take deposits from consumers. Investment banks rely on capital and loans from other institutions to fund their activities.

Next, the government went beyond its formal obligations to Freddie Mac and Fannie Mae, which consisted of a $2.25 billion line of credit to each firm. The problem was that as Freddie Mac and Fannie Mae began to report large losses from mortgage defaults, the good credit standing of the GSEs evaporated and they were forced to pay higher interest rates. The spread between GSE debt and Treasury debt, which had been as low as 10 basis points (one tenth of one percentage point), widened to over 100 basis points in July. The loss of confidence raised the cost of borrowing, which undermined the firms' profitability, which further reduced investor confidence, in a downward spiral.

On September 7, 2008, the Treasury placed Freddie Mac and Fannie Mae under "conservatorship." Under this arrangement, the government guaranteed a much broader range of GSE securities. The goal in the short run was to reduce the borrowing costs of the agencies (as of November of 2008, this goal had not been achieved, as GSE securities continued to bear a risk premium over Treasuries). The goal in the long run was to revisit the structure of the GSEs, with options ranging from keeping them substantially the same to making them more private to turning them into public utilities.

One week later, the investment bank Lehman Brothers was finished. Government officials tried to arrange a merger with another financial institution, but the government was unwilling to meet the demands of Barclays or Bank of America in terms of guarantees against losses from some of Lehman's portfolio. On September 15, Lehman was forced into bankruptcy. That same day, Merrill Lynch accepted a purchase offer from Bank of America, and it became clear that no investment bank was going to survive as an independent entity. Within a week, Goldman Sachs and Morgan Stanley obtained commercial bank charters.

It turned out that some large money market funds had significant holdings of short-term debt from Lehman. With Lehman bankrupt, at least one fund was forced to "break the buck," marking the value of its shares below one dollar. Given the way that money market funds had evolved into close substitutes for bank deposits, the Federal Reserve decided that a run on such funds had to be avoided, and it hastily set up a guarantee fund to reassure investors.

On Tuesday, September 16, shares of AIG, an insurance company that was a large seller of credit default swaps, lost 90 percent of their value. The Federal Reserve put together an $85 billion bailout, which subsequently had to be increased, as major counterparties to AIG demanded more collateral to back the credit default swaps.

The following weekend, Treasury Secretary Henry Paulson developed a proposal based on suggestions to handle the crisis with the equivalent of the Resolution Trust Corporation, which liquidated the assets of failed savings and loans in the 1980s. He proposed that $700 billion be used to purchase the mortgage-backed securities that he said were "clogging" the financial system. His reasoning was that once the banks were relieved of these assets of uncertain value, ordinary lending would resume.

Paulson's plan drew intense public opposition. On September 29, it was voted down in the U.S. House of Representatives. However, faced with sharp declines in stock prices and widespread pressure from the financial community, the House relented and a revised bailout bill cleared Congress on October 2.

Meanwhile the crisis had affected institutions around the world. European governments had been pressed to hastily enact deposit insurance for their threatened banks. However, Iceland's banks had accumulated too much in foreign liabilities for their government to cover, and the entire country was essentially bankrupt. Around the world, stock prices plummeted and major banks had to be merged or bailed out by governments.

Although the bailout legislation passed, the original Paulson plan was abandoned before a single mortgage-backed security was purchased. Instead, the Treasury deployed the first $250 billion under the plan to recapitalize banks by buying preferred stock. As of November, Congress and the Treasury had yet to determine the use of the remaining funds, but possibilities included investments in automobile manufacturers as well as more bank capitalization efforts.

The general rationale for the government's actions was that since the Great Depression was exacerbated by bank failures, preventing bank failures was necessary in order to prevent another Great Depression. This rationale was made credible by the fact that Federal Reserve Chairman Ben Bernanke is a scholar with expertise in the history of the Great Depression.

The macroeconomic theory pertaining to the response to the crisis is murky, at best. The most standard textbook economic model covers generic fiscal and monetary policy. That is, changes to government spending and tax policy, and interventions by the central bank to change the money supply and short-term interest rates. In the textbook depiction, there is no special role for policies to forestall a contraction in the financial sector.

There is no consensus concerning the macroeconomic impact of financial distress. There are no standard indicators of the existence of a credit crunch. On an ad hoc basis, several commentators seized on the interest rate spread between three-month Treasury securities and three-month inter-bank loan rates in the eurodollar market (the so-called TED spread) as an indicator. However, because this measures interest rates over a very short period, it is highly sensitive to small changes in default probabilities. If you are lending one million dollars for 10 years, an increase in the probability of default of one-tenth of one percent has almost no effect on the required interest rate. If you are lending money for three months, an increase in the default probability of one-tenth of one percent raises the required interest rate by about 40 basis points. Even when the TED rose to more than 400 basis points over its pre-crisis lows, this still represented an increase in default probabilities of only about one percent.

Even if there were an accepted method of measuring the extent of a credit crunch, there is no reliable estimate of the impact of a credit crunch on real economic activity. We do not know how much GDP will contract or unemployment will rise based on any given level of financial distress.

Finally, there is no body of economic theory that deals with the relief of financial distress. We do not know what is the best policy for providing credit to non-financial firms. Should government prop up failing banks, work through healthy banks, or skip the banks altogether and lend directly? Having no clear rationale for any of these, it might be best for government to do nothing. In fact, it could be argued that the government's inconsistent and clumsy efforts to intervene in financial markets simply added to the uncertainty of investors.

Economist Markus K. Brunnermeier noted that $8 trillion in stock market wealth was lost in the United States alone between October 2007 and October 2008, which far exceeds the losses in mortgage securities or in housing wealth.[13] Presumably, if the policy moves had been successful, the stock market reaction would have been less severe.

Overall, what strikes me both about the crisis and the response was that information was dispersed in such a way that decision-makers were not making good choices. The knowledge/power discrepancy was a factor throughout.

The scope of firms exceeded what could be prudently managed. At AIG insurance, for example, in retrospect it seems absurd that the business of selling credit default swaps was allowed to jeopardize all of the traditional lines of insurance. The latter appear to have been managed profitably, with reasonable margins of safety. They gave the company its overall AAA rating, which AIG proceeded to gamble away in its credit default swaps venture.

With traditional mortgage lending, knowledge and power are both dispersed. Banks would originate loans in their local markets, and ex-

---

[13] Markus K. Brunnermeier, "Deciphering the Liquidity and Credit Crunch 2007-08," paper prepared for a symposium in the *Journal of Economic Perspectives*. http://www.princeton.edu/~markus/research/papers/liquidity_credit_crunch.pdf

ecutives generally understood their business. When the industry changed to a model of indirect lending and securitization, the power in financial markets became highly centralized among the firms doing securitization—Fannie Mae, Freddie Mac, and the large investment banks. The valuable information about conditions in the origination markets, including the low quality of underwriting practices and the large numbers of people borrowing to buy houses that were beyond their capacity to afford, either failed to reach or failed to have an impact on key decision-makers.

Similarly, the response to the crisis appears to have suffered from a lack of information. Rather than being able to anticipate the interdependencies in financial markets, regulators seemed to be continually taken by surprise. Each week, a new firm or class of firms would come under market suspicion, and the Treasury and the Fed would implement a new emergency bailout for the immediate problem. They were never able to set up a firewall that could keep the crisis from spreading.

Needed: A Stern Sheriff

The crisis was in some respects similar to a bank run. As institutions lost confidence in the solvency of their counterparties in transactions such as repurchase agreements or credit default swaps, they demanded more collateral as protection. This increase in the demand for collateral further weakened the institutions, causing more counterparties to demand collateral, creating a vicious cycle.

I propose a metaphor for what was happening. Imagine a gambling parlor with several poker tables. The gamblers become wary and suspicious. Some of them stand up and start to shout and point fingers at one another. They say, "I do not have faith that you have the funds to cover your bets. Give me money now, before you run out." They start grabbing and pushing and shoving. Order breaks down, and the gambling parlor degenerates into an uncontrolled riot.

What is needed in this situation, in my opinion, is a stern sheriff. The sheriff needs to clap his hands on the gamblers' shoulders and say, "Boys, sit down and keep your hands to yourselves. We're going to get things settled out here, but you need to wait. Those of you who are patient and wait until we've got things sorted out will get most of what you are entitled. But those of you who are not patient and who push and grab will get a lot less."

With an uninsured bank, the stern sheriff approach could stop a bank run. Suppose that the bank has loans that are coming due in three months, but right now it is short of cash. The stern sheriff approach would be to charge a high fee for bank withdrawals now, with a much lower fee in three months when it expects loan repayments to give it plenty of cash on hand. Customers who participate in the run will be hit with high fees. Customers who wait three months will preserve more of their wealth.

Similarly, as the financial crisis unfolded, the government could have imposed penalties on firms that make extravagant demands for collateral to back repurchase agreements, credit default swaps, and similar instruments in this environment. These penalties would have helped deter the collateral demands. That in turn would have prevented, or at least relieved, the liquidity squeeze that took place.

Instead of the stern sheriff, we had Mr. Bernanke and Mr. Paulson running around with huge bags of money, frantically dumping it on the tables in the gambling parlor: $30 billion to cover Bear Stearns' bets, $100 billion to cover AIG's bets, $300 billion to cover Citigroup's bets, and so forth. This policy of trying to cover the gamblers' bets only served to agitate the situation. It rewarded the impatient, grab-it-while-you-can-get-it mindset that was driving the disorderly riot. The way I see it, we should have punished the impatient grabbers and instead rewarded firms that were willing to sit back and let the contracts play out.

Knowledge versus Power

When it comes to hindsight about why the financial crisis was not prevented, I would argue that the regulators suffered from a lack of knowledge. Had policymakers determined that the housing bubble posed risk, they could have warned banks and the GSEs to limit their risk exposure starting in, say, 2005. Had policymakers understood the way that bank capital requirements were distorting the mortgage market away from direct lending and toward securitization, they could have adjusted those capital requirements. Had regulators understood the extent to which the GSEs were trading off safety and soundness in order to meet affordable housing goals, they could have required the GSEs to change behavior, either by buying fewer risky loans or by raising more capital. Had regulators understood the way that rating agencies were mislabeling mortgage securities, they could have issued rules to banks requiring them to treat mortgage securities as riskier than their ratings signified.

The failure to regulate in time was not due to lack of tools. Nor was it due to lack of will, as is suggested by the narrative that a free-market ideology prevailed. The failure to prevent the crisis was due to the lack of knowledge among key policymakers. This discrepancy between knowledge and power is the central theme of this book.

I believe similarly that the failures in the private sector were also due largely to a discrepancy between power and knowledge. The leaders of financial firms did not set out to incur large risks for short-term gains, although that certainly is what resulted in many instances. Rather, the CEOs at banks and other firms believed that they were following sound, long-term strategies. From their perspective, they were using highly-rated securities in ways that met the approval of regulators who in turn had created a framework for safety and soundness. At lower levels, there were staff who were concerned that the risk/reward trade-offs were not being made correctly. Journalists and Congressional committees have uncovered warnings at the GSEs and at the rating agencies about problems. However, those warnings were delivered in a context in which CEOs were receiving other signals, particularly from their counterparts at other firms, which convinced them that risk was contained.

Finally, the response to the crisis continued to demonstrate a knowledge/power discrepancy. Henry Paulson seized the power to buy "toxic" assets. However, as soon as Congress gave him money and authority, it became apparent that his agency did not have the knowledge to undertake such a program.

We probably should not be surprised that the knowledge/power discrepancy arose. The next chapter focuses on the disparity between the trend toward diffuse, specialized knowledge and the trend toward concentrated political power.

Chapter 2
The Discrepancy Between Knowledge and Power

During the financial crisis of 2008, I coined the expression "suits vs. geeks divide" to describe what I saw as the discrepancy between knowledge and power within the financial sector. That is, top-level decision-makers at firms and regulatory agencies did not understand the new environment in which they were operating. Critical knowledge was instead located lower down in organizations, among the financial engineers, or "geeks."

I see the knowledge/power discrepancy as a generic problem not limited to financial services. Knowledge is becoming more specialized and more dispersed, while government power is becoming more concentrated. This discrepancy creates the potential for government to become increasingly erratic and unaccountable and, as a result, less satisfying to individuals.

This chapter first defines power as the ability to control actions of others. Power can be exercised by making decisions or through setting the incentives by which others make decisions. This is followed by a discussion of measures of knowledge and power, and a variety of indicators illustrating that knowledge is becoming more specialized. To gauge the concentration of political power, I examine spending per legislator as an indicator of trends.

Spending per legislator has increased because of both scale factors and scope factors. The scale of government rises as population per jurisdiction increases. The increased scope of government reflects the "bundling" of more and more services into the government "package," a process which is unchecked because of government's monopoly power. Overall, the increase in concentration of power raises questions about both efficiency and equity.

Political power is allocated by a "winners-take-most" tournament. This creates extreme inequality and puts ordinary individuals in the position of having to ingratiate themselves with political figures. The concentration of political power contrasts with the diffusion of specialized knowledge. Reformers, who seek to improve the effectiveness of government processes through better use of information age tools, fail to address the issue of concentration of power.

The Internet provides an alternative model of governance in which power is not concentrated. No single company or government body controls access to the Internet. An individual does not need to obtain official approval or a license of any kind to access content or make content available on the Internet. Instead, both information and power are diffuse. This suggests that concentration of power is not necessarily inevitable or desirable.

Power

Power is the ability to manage or design. People with power make decisions or design incentives that influence the actions of others. These decisions and incentives can have both intended and unintended consequences.

In addition to the intended and unintended consequences of power, there are two other important sources of outcomes and of economic change. One is external changes to the economic environment, including accidents, wars, and storms. The other factor is the evolutionary process. Market competition acts as a filter to sift through new technologies and new business methods.

As an example of design, suppose that an automobile manufacturer designs a bonus program for dealers that is based on sales volume. The incentives may have the intended consequence of raising sales volume. However, they may have an unintended consequence of encouraging dealers to sell lower priced models with low profit margins, because it is easier to increase sales of those cars.

Meanwhile, another source of change will be market evolution. This might lead domestic competitors to focus on lower volume, high margin cars, while foreign competitors start to enter the low price market. These evolutionary trends also affect the outcome of the incentive system put in place by our auto manufacturer.

The Basel agreement on international bank capital requirements is another example of management and consciously designed incentives. The Basel agreement had the intended consequence of reducing the willingness of banks to use short-term deposits to finance mortgage loans. In the wake of the savings and loan crisis, regulators were keenly aware of the risk of deposit finance for fixed-rate mortgages.

However, the Basel standards had the unintended consequence of encouraging banks to hold risky mortgage-backed securities. The evolution of market innovations, including credit scoring, sub-prime securitization, and credit default swaps, exacerbated these unintended consequences. Finally, the "storm" of the house price bubble and crash interacted with these developments to cause an outcome for the banking system that was the opposite of what the Basel standards were supposed to promote.

When people exercise power by making decisions or designing incentives, the knowledge they have is likely to affect the balance among intended consequences, unintended consequences, external events, and evolution. The more that the decision-maker knows about the domain of a decision, the more likely it is that intended consequences will flow from that decision, and the less likely it is that the outcome will differ sharply from what was planned.

What this framework suggests is that the quality of decisions depends on the relationship between knowledge and power. When knowledge is highly concentrated, power can be used effectively to make decisions that achieve intended results. On the other hand, when knowledge is dispersed, concentrated power can produce a brittle system in which mistakes are made frequently and corrected only with difficulty. With dispersed knowledge, decentralized systems, notably markets, are likely to be more robust than centralized organizations, such as large corporations or governments.

I believe that the relationship between knowledge and power currently favors decentralized systems. I have a strong intuitive sense that specialized knowledge is increasing, making knowledge more dispersed. However, this intuition is difficult to operationalize, measure, and document.

A big problem with trying to prove that specialized knowledge is increasing is that it requires a quantifiable definition of knowledge. I do not have such a definition, nor is one readily available, but perhaps I can justify my intuition by listing some examples.

One example is the number of specialties and sub-specialties in medicine. According to one study, the number of sub-specialties increased from about 30 in the early 1970s to about 100 in the late 1990s.[1]

Another example is the number of academic disciplines and sub-disciplines. In recent decades the number of majors and concentrations at universities has increased. Within economics, the field with which I am most familiar, new sub-specialties have emerged. An individual can now describe oneself as a game theorist or a behavioral economist or an experimental economist.

Yet another example is library classification systems. I believe that over time these numbering systems, especially the Library of Congress Classification System, have added more categories. Intuitively, this reflects more specific realms of knowledge.

Still another example is job classifications. In the United States, the number of people classified as "laborers" or "production workers" has declined. Instead, it seems that more occupations require specialized knowledge.

When I was in business, I was briefly involved in an effort to redesign our software infrastructure by applying a method known as in-

---

[1] Fred Donini-Lenhoff and Hannah Hedrick, "Growth of Specialization in Graduate Medical Education," *Journal of the American Medical Association* 284 (2000):1284–1289.

formation engineering. One component of information engineering is to define every entity used in a business process. Examples of entities might be: customer, invoice, product SKU, etc. The complexity of the business might be measured by the number of distinct entities or the number of entity relationships (an invoice is related to a customer as well as to a product SKU). My conjecture is that if information engineering were applied to the economy as a whole, the complexity would be far greater today than it was years ago.

Northwestern University's Benjamin Jones has come up with a number of metrics that bear on the issue of specialization.[2] Using a database of patent registrations, Jones developed several indicators, including: team size (the number of inventors listed on each patent); time lag (the delay between consecutive patent applications from the same inventor); the number of previous patents cited, extended to include the entire tree (citations of citations, etc.); and age at first innovation.

Jones found that all of these indicators showed an increase in what he calls "the burden of knowledge," meaning the effort required to accumulate enough knowledge to file for a new patent. It takes more people to accumulate the knowledge, and it takes each person more time to accumulate knowledge, presumably because of greater specialization.

Another indicator of increased specialization is the additional use of trade and markets. In the eighteenth century, an American colonial family was likely to grow some of its own food, build its own home, and sew its own clothes. Over the next century, Americans increasingly began to produce goods for sale in the market and to obtain food, clothing, and shelter from the market.

In 1880, building a house required few skills that were out of the reach of an ordinary individual. Today, building a house requires knowledge of electrical systems, heating and air conditioning systems, plumbing systems, and other specialized expertise.

In the first half of this century, many men were general laborers in factories and on farms. Women were general laborers as well, doing

[2] Benjamin Jones, "The Burden of Knowledge and the 'Death of the Renaissance Man': Is Innovation Getting Harder?" http://www.kellogg.northwestern.edu/faculty/jones-ben/htm/BurdenOfKnowledge.pdf

housework and preparing meals. Today, fewer than 10 percent of Americans are classified as manufacturing production workers or farm laborers. Women participate more in the market labor force, and most of our meals are prepared either in fast food restaurants or in convenience foods sold at supermarkets.

Law has become more specialized. Business contracts, for example, require increasingly specific expertise to write. Legal practices now emphasize more particular sub-specialties than they did 50 years ago.

News media have become more specialized. General-interest news media, such as newspapers, weekly news magazines, and network television, have been losing market share. Meanwhile, new media are gaining: Web sites and blogs aimed at particular industrial niches, professional sub-specialties, or narrow audiences are increasing their readership. Chris Anderson's *The Long Tail* documents the way that the Internet has promoted the growth of these niche markets.

Suppose that one were trying to dispute the notion that knowledge has become increasingly specialized. What sort of evidence might indicate that knowledge specialization has declined or remained constant? It seems to me that if knowledge is not more specialized, then we should encounter people today who appear to be as broadly skilled as Leonardo da Vinci was in the fifteenth century. That is, we should occasionally observe someone who is a leading scholar in many scientific and artistic disciplines. Instead, we credit someone as a "renaissance person" who is conversant in several fields, even if he or she is not a leader in any one field.

Another observation we should be able to make if knowledge has not become more specialized is that knowledge is rapidly disappearing. That is, given that new fields of knowledge are being created, the only way that specialization could remain constant would be if other fields of knowledge were declining with equal rapidity. The list of products and skills that have disappeared over the past century should be as long as the list of products and skills that have newly emerged.

We certainly have added fields of knowledge that did not exist years ago. If we have not subtracted an equal number of fields of knowledge, then it would seem that we necessarily have become more specialized. For example, in medicine, it does not seem that as many specialties have disappeared over the past 50 years as have emerged. Instead, the proportion of physicians in general practice has declined.

Along these lines, try to imagine becoming a generalist. One can argue that as of 400 years ago, it was possible for a single individual to understand what was then known about every scientific subject or to read every book. One hundred years ago, it might have been possible to master all of what was known at the time about physics. Fifty years ago, an auto mechanic might have been able to fix any car on the road. None of these is possible today.

In 1995, I knew all of the techniques that were available for formatting content on the World Wide Web. By 2000, the majority of the top Web sites used techniques with which I was completely unfamiliar. Today, no one person can possibly master all of the techniques for formatting Web content.

How can specialized knowledge be combined to make good decisions? In business, this is one of the issues involved in deciding what will be included in the scope of a firm and what will be undertaken in a market. Should an automobile company manufacture its own tires? Should it manage and operate an on-site cafeteria for production workers?

In management consulting jargon, a firm is said to have a "core competence," meaning something that it does better than any other firm. The question is whether the firm should engage in activities that are beyond its core competence. Typically, the management consultant's advice is to stay away from such activities, and instead to outsource them to other firms. When a firm elects to obtain a service or a component from external sources, it is using the market. An automobile company that purchases tires from a supplier is conceding that tire production requires specialized knowledge that the automobile company cannot obtain and manage effectively internally.

There is a considerable literature in economics concerning what sets the scope of the firm. For example, Ronald Coase suggested that transaction costs would be the determining factor.[3] Does it cost more for the auto manufacturer to interact with the tire market or to organize and monitor the internal production of tires? If the auto company manufactures its own tires, it has to manage the incentive system and performance of the workers. If it purchases tires from a supplier, it pays the supplier to solve those problems. Coase argued that whichever structure would emerge would minimize the total cost of managing the tire manufacturing process and managing the relationship between the auto company and the tire manufacturer. When managing the relationship is relatively expensive, it would make sense to internalize tire manufacturing. On the other hand, when managing the internal production system for tires is relatively expensive for the automobile manufacturer to perform, then it would make sense to outsource the function.

Each individual firm chooses which functions to manage internally and which functions to outsource to the market. However, in a competitive economy, one would expect cost-minimizing structures to emerge. A firm that keeps a function in-house even when it is costly to do so will be driven out of business by a firm that outsources functions that are more effectively managed externally.

I want to return to the distinction between managerial design and evolution. Even when a firm uses an external supplier, it may still apply managerial design. If the firm imposes specific contractual requirements on the supplier, then that is a managed process. In contrast, a market process is one in which firms shop for goods and services. If a bank contracts with a software company to build a specific human resources system, that is a managed process. If instead the bank obtains an off-the-shelf human resources system, that is a market process.

In practice, use of management and use of markets is not a binary distinction. There is a continuum of possibilities. In-house production would be at the management end of the continuum. Having a specific, detailed contractual relationship with an outside supplier would be close to the management end. Choosing from among various suppliers

---

[3] Ronald H. Coase, "The Nature of the Firm," *Economica* 4 (1937): 386–405.

based on an evaluation of how well the supplier's product fits the firm's needs would be close to the market end. Obtaining supplies by purchasing generic products primarily on the basis of price would be even further on the market end of the spectrum.

Managerial design works well at incorporating centralized knowledge. Markets work well at incorporating decentralized knowledge. Therefore, the boundaries of a firm are likely to be knowledge boundaries. When decisions can be made with relatively few unintended consequences and little need to respond to random events or evolutionary developments, internal management and design are appropriate. When lack of knowledge means that unintended consequences will be proportionately large or that random shocks and evolutionary developments require frequent adaptation, external markets are likely to be more effective.

If knowledge has become more specialized, then my expectation would be that the scope of an individual firm would tend to decrease. Each unit in the economy will engage in fewer different activities. Note, however, that the scale of a firm might increase. Choosing a smaller scope means fewer activities, but it does not necessarily imply a smaller organization.

As an economy becomes more specialized, household production goes down and market consumption goes up. Instead of spending a lot of time preparing food, consumers take more meals in restaurants and purchase more prepared foods from supermarkets. Instead of spending time laundering and ironing clothes, consumers will employ washing machines, laundry services, and permanent-press fabrics.

Similarly, as the economy becomes more specialized, in-house production within firms would decrease. Thirty years ago, when a business needed a program to store and retrieve data, its computer programmers wrote all of the software code themselves. Today, firms no longer write data retrieval programs from scratch. Instead, they use generic database software. In general, firms are outsourcing many functions, including data centers, call centers, and human resource functions.

With specialization of knowledge, large scale has advantages, but broad scope has disadvantages. Being highly competent in one area has value. Making decisions outside of one's area of competence is more likely to cause problems.

Increased Concentration of Government Power

Government power has become more concentrated over time. Despite large increases in population, we have the same governmental units—50 states and 1 Congress—at work. Thus, the scale of government has gone up. At the same time, the scope of government has increased. Government is involved in more activities than ever before.

Perhaps the most dramatic illustration of the concentration of government power can be seen in the spectacular bailouts undertaken in 2008. The $700 billion Troubled Asset Relief Program (TARP) gave the Treasury Secretary unprecedented authority to spend an enormous sum of money over a short period of time with wide discretion. In fact none of the money was spent in the manner that was indicated when the bill was being debated. At that time, the plan was to purchase mortgage securities. Instead, most of the initial allocation was used to purchase preferred stock in banks.

The financial rescue program was never supported by the American public. Prior to the first vote on the Emergency Economic Stabilization Act that authorized the TARP, Congressmen were reporting constituent mail running nine to one against the idea. As of December of 2008, when proposals were floated to divert some TARP funds to bailing out domestic automobile manufacturers, polls showed a majority of Americans opposed. If the public was opposed to an auto industry rescue, it seems safe to assume that opposition to the financial industry bailouts remained high. TARP was not a policy that was forced on Congress from below. It was instead imposed by the elites on a skeptical public.

The TARP represents a remarkable expansion of government power. Ordinarily, one might expect that such a dramatic political action would be undertaken only with a strong consensus of public support. The fact that it was carried out in the face of significant, even overwhelming opposition on the part of the general public makes it quite breathtaking.

Economists and others who look at trends in the distribution of income have raised questions about increases in the inequality of income and wealth. What I am suggesting is that similar questions can be raised about the increased concentration of political power. How should we measure the power of individual politicians? Do too few politicians have too much power? What could be done to redistribute political power? What would be the benefits and costs of doing so?

When it comes to the concentration of income and wealth, we have these sorts of conversations all the time. The standard measures of economic well-being reveal a distribution that is highly skewed. Indeed, this is so obvious that I use it to teach high school students the basic concepts of mean, median, and skewness. I say, "Suppose that the richest person in our neighborhood moved out, and Bill Gates moved in. Would the *median* wealth per household in our neighborhood go up? (No.) Would the *mean* wealth per household in our neighborhood go up? (Yes, by a lot.) Would the wealth distribution in our neighborhood become more skewed? (Yes, by a lot.)"

Most people think that it is better for the income distribution to be relatively equal than highly skewed. But there are other issues involved. A classic economic title on the subject is *Equality and Efficiency: The Big Trade-off*, by Arthur Okun. Okun argues that while we might prefer both more efficiency and more equality, often those goals conflict. This provides a framework for evaluating policies.

For example, suppose that cutting capital gains tax rates would make the economy more productive on average but lead to a more skewed income distribution. We might call such a policy a move to the right along the trade-off. Going in the other direction, raising capital gains tax rates would be a move to the left. Or, suppose that a policy of replacing farm crop price supports with means-tested grants to farmers would improve both equality and efficiency. If so, then we could call such a policy a pure winner. Finally, suppose that providing subsidized flood insurance for million-dollar homes on the coast is adverse for both equality and efficiency. If so, then we could call such a policy a pure loser.

A number of economists have pointed out that over the past 30 years our economy has become more efficient (as indicated by higher average productivity) while the distribution of income and wealth has become less equal. This suggests that we have made a move to the right. Perhaps this means that policy ought to aim at moving back in the other direction.

In fact, one rationale for greater centralization of political power is that we may want concentrated political power to serve as a check on concentrated economic power. However, I think that it would be a mistake to conclude that this rationale is sufficient to end the conversation about political power. There are a number of theoretical and empirical holes that need to be filled in.

For one thing, over the past 30 years, while we have witnessed an increase in the concentration of wealth, we have also seen the concentration of political power rise, at least according to the measures that will be used in this book. If the political concentration was supposed to fix the economic concentration, it does not seem to have worked.

At this point, it is appropriate to recall another elementary statistical concept, the difference between correlation and causation. We have three phenomena—greater efficiency, greater economic inequality, and increased concentration of political power—that are correlated. We do not know the directions of causality, if any.

One plausible explanation for greater efficiency and greater economic inequality is the computer revolution. In 1998, economists Claudia Goldin and Lawrence Katz gave this the name *skill-biased technological change*. They suggested that computers were increasing the productivity of highly educated workers more rapidly than that of poorly educated workers. If there are barriers to obtaining a college education (such as inadequate high school preparation, which could in turn be subject to barriers established by individual cognitive ability), then skill-biased technological change will lead to increasing inequality, even as it enhances overall economic efficiency.

(In their recent book *The Race Between Education and Technology*, Goldin and Katz argue that the skill bias in technological change has grown at a fairly steady rate for the past 100 years. They see a slowdown in educational attainment over the past 30 years. This might help to explain the rise in income inequality in recent years, but it makes the acceleration in productivity that took place in the 1990s somewhat of a puzzle.)

It could be that over the past 30 years, public policy tried to move along the great trade-off to the left, but skill-biased technological change was more powerful in moving along the trade-off to the right. By the same token, it could be that greater concentration of political power served as a check on concentration of wealth, but skill-biased technological change was more powerful in causing the concentration of wealth to increase.

The point I am making here is that concentration of political power and concentration of economic power are not simple phenomena. There are complexities at the conceptual and empirical levels. Given the complexities, I believe that having conversations about these issues is valuable. However, it is not wise to leap to conclusions based on just one or two stylized facts.

Here are some more questions that might stimulate useful conversations:

- Is Arthur Okun's framework also useful for looking at political power? Perhaps there is a big trade-off between efficiency and equality when it comes to political power. If larger units execute the functions of government more effectively but are more remote from the typical citizen, this would create such a trade-off.

- Are larger, centralized governmental units more cost-effective than smaller, decentralized governmental units? If not, then there is no trade-off. If decentralized government means better government (including providing a better check against concentrated economic power), then that would tend to suggest that concentration of political power is undesirable.

- How is political power acquired and retained? In the case of wealth, we worry that inherited wealth creates unequal opportunity. We ask whether there is mobility up the economic ladder or whether people remain stuck at the bottom. Similarly, one may ask whether access to political power is fairly restricted or whether the competition for political positions is relatively open.

- What are the consequences of political inequality for overall social inequality? The very rich lead different lifestyles from the rest of us. Do the very powerful also experience life on a day-to-day basis in ways that differ drastically from ordinary individuals?

Spending per Legislator

One crude measure of the concentration of political power is spending per legislator. I noticed this when it struck me that Montgomery County, Maryland, where I live, has a budget of $4.3 billion, which is allocated by a nine-member County Council. Dividing the budget by the number of legislators gives almost $500 million in spending per legislator, every year. That struck me as considerable power for individuals.

$500 million to spend each year is a lot of money. *Forbes* reported that in 2007, only four executives were paid as much as $100 million. The highest-paid executive, Larry Ellison, received $193 million in compensation.[4] Looking at cumulative pay over the past five years, only two executives—Steve Jobs of Apple and Ray Irani of Occidental Petroleum ($661 million and $550 million, respectively)—received more in compensation than the average spending of a Montgomery County Council member in one year. Using a different methodology, the *New York Times* reported that Ellison received only $61 million, and that he was the second-highest paid executive, with Merrill Lynch's John Thain receiving $84 million.

If you had a fortune of $10 billion and earned five percent in interest, this would give you $500 million per year to spend. Igor Zyuzin, just above 84th place on the *Forbes* list of the world's billionaires, has $10 billion in net worth. Several others are tied with Zyuzin for 77th

---

[4] *Forbes*, April 30, 2008. http://www.forbes.com/lists/2008/12/lead_bestbosses08_CEO-Compensation_Rank.html

place on the *Forbes* list.[5] In other words, only 83 people in the world, including only 28 American citizens, have as much wealth at their disposal as a member of the Montgomery County Council.

Two factors—population per jurisdiction and spending per capita—have caused government power to scale up dramatically over the past 40 years. Whether we look at the nine-member Montgomery County Council or the U.S. Congress, the budgetary powers are far higher than they were just a generation ago.

Unchecked and Unbalanced

One objection to treating spending per legislator as a measure of government power is that it ignores the checks and balances in the budget-setting process. In reality, the fact that spending per legislator is $5.5 billion at the Federal level does not mean that any given House member absolutely controls $5.5 billion.

The closest thing to absolute Budget control by an individual legislator is the Congressional "earmark." Citizens Against Government Waste estimates that earmarks in fiscal year 2008 totaled $17.2 billion.[6] Divided by 535 Congressmen and Senators, this is an average of just over $30 million per legislator that is spent "free and clear." Although this is tiny within the context of the overall Budget, $30 million is still a pretty nice chunk of change for one person to have at his or her disposal each and every year. According to the Tax Policy Center, as reported by Paul Krugman, the 99.9th percentile in the U.S. income distribution was about $1.7 million.[7] He estimates the 99.99th percentile as something over $6 million. Control over earmark spending alone makes U.S. legislators able to spend much more than that.

Some reformers have argued that political campaigns ought to be publicly financed. I think we have a lot of public election funding

---

[5] *Forbes*, March 5, 2008. http://www.forbes.com/2008/03/05/worlds-richest-billion aires-billionaires08-cx_lk_0305all_slide_76.html?thisSpeed=30000

[6] Citizens Against Government Waste. http://www.cagw.org/site/PageServer?page-name=reports_pigbook2008

[7] Paul Krugman, "Graduates vs. Oligarchs," *New York Times*, February 27, 2006.

already—it just all goes to the incumbents. Presumably, most earmarks are used to benefit people who are eligible to vote for the legislator. If a Congressman is up for re-election every other year and has $30 million per year in earmarks, then in one election cycle the Congressman will have spent $60 million in public funds on re-election efforts. The total of $17.2 billion in earmarks is more than 10 times the sum spent on efforts to unseat incumbent legislators. (A story in *USA Today* quotes the Center for Responsive Politics as saying that $2.6 billion was raised for the 2006 mid-term elections.[8] Presumably, much of that went to incumbents rather than to their opponents.)

I do not have a comparable estimate for earmarks in Montgomery County. However, a case could be made that in enacting the entire $4.3 billion budget the County Council is unchecked and unbalanced. All nine members of the County Council belong to the same political party.

The County Council has always been controlled by the party in the past. As in China, citizens assume that the party will be in control for the foreseeable future as well. As in China, wealthy real estate developers must have cozy relationships with the party.

The party always wins because key voting blocs are kept happy, as described by the *Washington Post*.[9] Even while its tax base was shrinking due to housing market woes, the story notes that for public sector unions, "Recent labor contracts provide most workers with salary increases of 26 to 29 percent over three years, including 8 percent this fiscal year for most general government workers."

Subsequent stories reported that attempts to trim these increases in view of the fiscal crisis were defeated. The party satisfied its voting blocs.

---

[8] Barbara Borst, "Campaign spending up in U.S. congressional elections," *USA Today*, October 29, 2006. http://www.usatoday.com/news/washington/2006-10-29-campaign-spending_x.htm

[9] Ann E. Marimow, "Union Influence Sways Montgomery Budget Talks," *Washington Post*, May 10, 2008. http://www.washingtonpost.com/wp-dyn/content/article/2008/05/10/AR2008051002592.html

The same *Washington Post* story points out that in 2002, two incumbents were defeated in an intra-party purge because they voted against the wishes of the public-sector unions. Otherwise, incumbents handily defeat anyone from the opposition party, the locally moribund Republicans. The Republicans have no standing whatsoever with the unions, who are unmatched in their political activism and funding capabilities.

As it turns out, many local jurisdictions are, like Montgomery County, one-party jurisdictions. David Schleicher points out that in local elections people engage in automatic party-line voting based on national preferences.[10] Thus, unless the residents of a municipality change their national allegiance, there is no party competition in local elections. As a result, he argues,

> local government does not meet the most basic definitions of democracy—it does not provide voters with the ability to replace incumbents with opponents with different views and to have their views represented in local policies.

Comparison with Other Large Counties

The five largest counties in the country (leaving aside Harris County in Texas, which is governed as the city of Houston), and their populations and spending figures are as follows:

County	population (millions)	legislators	budget ($billions)	budget per legislator ($billions)
Los Angeles	9.90	5	$22.5	$4.5
Cook	5.30	17	3.2	0.2
Maricopa (Pho)	3.90	5	2.3	0.5
Orange (LA)	3.00	5	6.6	1.3
San Diego	3.00	5	4.7	0.9

[10] David Schleicher, "Why Is There No Partisan Competition in City Council Elections?: The Role of Election Law," *Journal of Law and Politics* 15 (2008). http://papers.ssrn.com/sol3/papers.cfm?abstract_id=1122422#PaperDownload

Five counties with populations similar to Montgomery County are the following:

County	population (millions)	legislators	budget ($billions)	budget per legislator ($billions)
Westchester	1.00	17	1.8	0.1
Milwaukee	1.00	19	1.4	0.1
Montgomery	0.90	9	4.3	0.5
DuPage (Ill)	0.90	18	0.4	0.0
Pinellas (Fl)	0.90	7	2	0.3

(Data sources: for county populations, Wikipedia, accessed June 20, 2008. For number of legislators and budgets, the Web sites of the individual counties.)

Montgomery County is somewhat atypical. Other counties of comparable size tend to have $100 million in spending per legislator, which is only about one-fifth of the spending of Montgomery County legislators. But $100 million per year is still more than the highest-paid CEO in the United States receives.

Comparison with States

One reason that Montgomery County, Maryland has such a high ratio of spending per legislator is that it is located next to Washington, DC. The Federal government enriches the surrounding area, so that Montgomery County is, along with Fairfax County and Arlington County, Virginia, one of the wealthiest counties in the United States.

In fact, the entire state of South Dakota has a budget of only $3 billion, compared with Montgomery County's $4.3 billion. South Dakota also has a somewhat lower population, with 767,000 residents, compared with an estimated one million in Montgomery County.[11]

Because South Dakota has 35 districts in its state senate and 70 districts in its state house, spending per legislator in the state is only

[11] All state figures are from Kaiser Permanente's "statehealthfacts.org" at www.statehealth-facts.org

$28 million. In fact, of all 50 states, only California, with $1.4 billion in spending per legislator, has a higher ratio than Montgomery County. California has 40 state senate districts and 80 state house districts, which is fewer than North Dakota, even though California's population is 36 million while North Dakota's population is well under 1 million.

The state with the lowest level of spending per legislator is New Hampshire because the state house has 400 members. Spending per legislator is only $11 million there. The next lowest state is North Dakota, which has 49 senate districts and 98 house districts with a budget of $3.3 billion. That works out to spending per legislator of $22 million. Overall, only fourteen states spend less than $100 million per legislator, and only Idaho, Maine, Montana, New Hampshire, North Dakota, South Dakota, and Vermont spend less than $50 million per legislator.

Generally speaking, spending per legislator is higher in states with higher populations. That is because most states have about 50 state senators and about 100 state representatives, regardless of population, and spending per capita tends to be fairly similar across states.

Criticizing this Measure of Power

There are a number of flaws with using budget per legislator as a measure of power. As noted, a legislator cannot act alone. Furthermore, legislators are subject to electoral challenge, even if it is only within their own party. It can be argued that much spending is "automatic," in that it is unrealistic that the current legislature could alter such spending. (On the other hand, "automatic" spending resulted from a decision at some point in time. Some of the automatic spending is of recent vintage, e.g., the prescription drug coverage for Medicare that was enacted during the George W. Bush Administration.)

One might argue that spending per legislator underestimates the power of legislators. They also can enact mandates, laws, and regulations that do not directly increase spending but still exert authority over citizens.

It is often argued that other loci of power have grown. These include courts, the executive branch, multinational corporations, and even individuals. The accusations about the judiciary include "legislating from the bench." The accusations about the executive include the "imperial Presidency." Many who write on globalization focus on the increased power of transnational actors, including corporations. The "superstar" phenomenon, in which the most successful individuals in entertainment, sports, and corporate leadership garner a strikingly large share of income, has accelerated.

Certainly, it is possible that *relative* to these other power centers, the power of legislatures has not increased over the last 40 years. Perhaps it has even declined.

Nonetheless, the factual point remains: Adjusted for inflation, the budgets of Federal, state, and local governments have surged. The number of representatives voting on each budget has stayed essentially the same. The number of constituents per legislator has risen, diluting the significance of an individual vote. The result has been to put more money at the disposal of a basically fixed number of legislators.

Regardless of whether one regards the increase in spending per legislator as a useful measure of political power, one may still ask: Is it a good thing? If we had the "right" ratio 40 years ago, do we have too much spending per legislator today? Alternatively, if we have the "right" ratio today, did we have too little spending per legislator 40 years ago?

Scale Creep and Scope Creep

Our political system is characterized by scale creep and scope creep. Scale creep means that fixed governmental units serve ever-larger populations. Scope creep means that government at all levels engages in more activities each decade.

When the United States was founded, its population was less than 4 million. There were 13 states, each with its own legislature. The U.S. Congress consisted of 65 Representatives and 26 Senators.

For the next century, much of America's population growth went to new states. This meant that new legislatures were being created,

thereby restraining the growth in the number of constituents per legislator. Congress expanded, until in 1910, with a population of 92 million, there were 435 Representatives and 92 Senators. For the past
100 years, the size of Congress has remained the same, apart from the
addition of Senators from Arizona, New Mexico, Hawaii, and Alaska.
Meanwhile, the nation's population has more than tripled.

The scale of government is completely different than what it was in
1790 or even in 1910. In 1790, there were fewer than 50,000 people per
legislator (dividing the population of 4 million by a total of 91 Representative and Senators). In 1910, there were fewer than 200,000 people
per legislator. Today, there are more than 500,000 people per legislator.

Los Angeles County, the largest county in America, has a population of 9.9 million, with a legislature consisting of five members.
Thus, the local government has almost 2 million people per legislator.

At each level of government, the number of legislators has remained
largely fixed while population has increased. The result is to increase
the number of constituents per legislator. It would seem that this has
to shift the balance of power away from the individual constituent.
Meanwhile, the scope of government also has increased. All levels of
government are involved in more activities than was the case historically.
For many years, the Constitution was interpreted as providing clear
boundaries between powers that were given to the Federal government
and powers that were left to the states. There was relatively little overlap.
Today, there appear to be few effective boundaries separating the responsibilities of the Federal government and the states. Both are involved in education, labor regulation, health care, income redistribution,
housing, insurance, security, and emergency assistance.

For example, public education used to be a state and local function, but increasingly, the Federal government is involved in providing
funding and setting standards for primary education. Similarly, the
regulation of carbon emissions in order to address climate change is
sometimes considered to be a problem that goes beyond the ability of
any one nation to regulate. It seemingly requires an international solution. Yet California attempted to establish standards for carbon
emissions from automobiles sold in that state.

We have had an individual state attempting to adopt auto emission standards for carbon dioxide with a goal of addressing global climate change. Meanwhile, we have the Federal government directing state and local policies in a number of areas, such as girls' scholastic athletics, with compliance required if the school wishes to receive its allotment of Federal funding.

It used to be that no level of government was engaged with the issue of adult smoking. Today, smokers are subject to Federal, state, and local regulation. Attempts to upgrade the nation's infrastructure for electricity generation and transmission also must deal with regulations at all three levels of government.

Jurisdictional issues create a number of anomalies. For example, employer-provided health insurance is regulated at the Federal level, but individual health insurance is regulated at the state level. We began with a Constitution that was interpreted as a device for carefully dividing political power among the various branches and levels of government. What has evolved is a system in which power is exercised at multiple levels and by various branches. Thus, we have had cases where courts have forced changes in school budgets. We have had regulatory agencies in the Executive Branch engage in what amounts to legislation. We have had legislators impose sentencing guidelines on courts.

One way to measure the scope of government is in terms of spending per person, in year 2000 dollars. By this measure, for our first 100 years, at the Federal level spending was under $100 per person. The table below shows real Federal spending every 10 years, starting in 1911.

Year	Federal spending per person, in year 2000 $
1911	$106
1921	$386
1931	$281
1941	$987
1951	$1,796
1961	$2,561
1971	$3,575
1981	$5,064
1991	$6,305
2001	$6,466

At the state and local level, real spending per person rose from $487 in 1931 to $1,148 in 1961 to $4,748 in 2001. Since 1961, the acceleration in real spending per capita has actually been higher at the state and local level than at the Federal level.

The Bundling of Government

What I am calling scope creep is similar to the economic concept known as bundling. Government engages in what economists call bundling, or aggregating goods and services into a package. As a consumer, you are familiar with bundling when it comes to cable television, where you are offered packages to choose from, even though many consumers might prefer a more discrete set of choices.

There is considerable economic literature on bundling.[12] The role of bundling in government has been discussed by Robert J. Mackay and Carolyn L. Weaver.[13]

As a taxpayer, you pay for a standard bundle of government services. You pay for government schools, whether you want them or not. You pay for government to conduct foreign policy, whether you agree with it or not. One way to reduce the concentration of political power would be to permit unbundling of government services.

In the private sector, firms engage in bundling in order to increase market share and spread fixed costs. However, competition often forces firms to unbundle their products, usually to the benefit of consumers. In the private sector, goods and services come bundled in a variety of ways. For example, a consumer can buy milk by the pint, by the quart, or by the gallon. However, if you need one-fourth of one cup of milk for a recipe, you will not be able to go to the store and buy milk in that amount. You will have to buy a larger amount. I would term this bundling by *volume*. In general, bundling by volume tends to be the most innocuous form of bundling.

[12] See, for example: William James Adams and Janet L. Yellin, "Commodity Bundling and the Burden of Monopoly," *Quarterly Journal of Economics* Vol. 90, No. 3 (1976): 475–498.

[13] Robert J. Mackay and Carolyn L. Weaver, "Commodity Bundling and Agenda Control in the Public Sector," *The Quarterly Journal of Economics* Vol. 98, No. 4 (1983): 611–635.

When you buy a computer, it comes with software. This is an example of what might be called *vertical* bundling. Two products that are highly complementary to one another are bundled together. When a razor is sold together with a combination of razor blades, this is another example of what I am calling vertical bundling.

I recently purchased a digital camera, which has many features that I am unlikely to use. These extra features, which have no value to me but which nonetheless are included with the camera, might be termed *horizontal* bundling.

Cable television exhibits all three types of bundling. Subscribers typically pay a fixed monthly charge, regardless of how much television they watch. This is bundling by volume. A subscription to cable television covers both the physical provision of the service (the wires to your home and the devices that send signals over those wires) and the content of the service (the channels that your home receives). That is vertical bundling. Finally, to the annoyance of many cable subscribers, they receive packages of channels, and it is often impossible to add or delete channels from a set package. This is horizontal bundling.

Significant bundling takes place in markets that are not highly competitive. Often, there is an element of "natural monopoly," in which fixed costs are high. A major purpose of bundling is to enable the seller to extract more revenues from the consumers with the greatest desire for the service, without losing revenues from those consumers with minimal desire for the service. The technical term for this is price discrimination.

The cable television provider puts certain channels into "premium" packages because the provider believes that people who are willing to pay more for cable television will choose those packages. At the same time, it believes that the "basic" package will appeal to even those consumers with very little desire for cable television. Offering different packages at different prices allows the cable provider to discriminate between customers with varying degrees of need for the service.

Cell phone service providers use volume bundles to try to retain low-volume users while obtaining more revenue from high-volume users. The high-volume user is offered a package with more minutes and a higher monthly fee. On a per-minute basis, heavy users receive a discount. However, heavy users cover a higher proportion of fixed costs than do modest users. The bundling that we observe in the cell phone market takes place because the fixed costs of setting up a cell network are high relative to the variable costs incurred when a customer uses the network. Once you have the network built, the cost of sending the signals is low.

If the cost of setting up a network were low relative to the cost of sending signals, then bundling would disappear from the cell phone market. Bundling tends to drive down the per-minute price to the consumer. This would make no sense if the (variable) cost per minute of sending signals were high compared with the (fixed) cost of setting up the network. If cell phone firms had to worry most about recovering variable costs, they would tend to charge the same per-minute fee for all users. They would have no incentive to offer volume discounts of any sort.

Given the actual structure of costs in the cell phone industry, you can charge a very low price per minute and still make money on each call. The trick is to get customers to subscribe to plans, and thereby to cover your fixed costs. Hence we have bundling.

Why doesn't the cable TV company charge for each channel? Why doesn't the cell phone company charge per minute? The reason is that those sorts of pricing policies would lose too many premium customers. If premium cable subscribers were not offered discount packages, many of them would revert to basic service and get their additional entertainment in other ways (by renting movies, for example). Similarly, if your cell phone service did not offer discount packages to high-volume users, those users would shift to Internet phones, land lines, or other cell phone providers.

Again, the purpose of bundling is to cover high fixed costs. If most of a firm's costs are fixed, then the firm wants to get as much revenue as it can. The goal is to get at least some revenue from the low-demand customers, and in addition to try to extract a premium from high-demand customers. When the cost consists mostly of labor time and materials, we are less likely to see bundling. Although it is not unheard-of for lawyers, accountants, barbers, or gasoline stations to offer "package deals," bundling is not nearly as widespread for those goods and services as it is for telecommunications services or for "information goods."

Government provides many services for which fixed costs are high relative to variable costs. For example, consider national defense. Once you have a military that is capable of protecting some of the population against foreign attack, the cost of protecting an additional citizen against foreign attack is almost zero. Law enforcement services also have a high element of fixed cost. However, once a court system is set up and police have been trained, the marginal cost of providing an additional citizen with the benefits of these services is low.

Nonetheless, many government services are labor-intensive. For example, in Montgomery County, Maryland, over 85 percent of the school budget is labor compensation. Garbage collection and road maintenance are other examples of labor-intensive services.

In markets where fixed costs are not overwhelming, competitive forces tend to drive out bundling. For example, the Internet has lowered the fixed cost associated with delivering information. This has put tremendous pressure on the newspaper and music industries. One no longer needs a large manufacturing plant and distribution network in order to be in the news or music business.

The newspaper bundles are being attacked from several directions. The most lucrative component of the bundle, the classified advertising section, faces competition from eBay, Craigslist, and a variety of employment search sites on the Web. Some traditional newspaper sections, such as sports or business, face competition from specialized cable channels and Web sites. Opinion pages face competition from political blogs and other narrowly-focused Web sites.

Bundling of services by government lacks economic justification. There is nothing efficient about combining public safety, health insurance, and agricultural policy. *Government bundles not because it should, but because it can. In fact, scope creep almost certainly reduces the efficiency of government.*

The effect of scale creep and scope creep is multiplicative, in the sense that total spending per legislator is equal to population per legislator times spending per person. Between 1951 and 2001, population doubled and per capita spending more than tripled. As a result, real spending per legislator at the Federal level went from $486 million to over $3.4 billion, nearly a seven-fold increase. Similar increases in concentration of power have taken place at the state and local levels.

It would appear that what has evolved represents a major imbalance of power. On the one hand, we have political units with relatively few elected officials controlling large amounts of spending. Recall Montgomery County, where spending per legislator is almost half a billion dollars per year. These nine relatively minor elected officials have control over much more than the annual earnings of all but the very richest people in the world. On the other hand, we have individuals who make up an infinitesimal portion of the voting population.

It is possible for a modern society to function without such a severe imbalance of power. In the cantons of Switzerland, for example, spending per legislator is far lower than in the United States, even though spending per capita is higher.

The population of Switzerland is about 7.5 million, and there are 26 cantons. Thus, a canton corresponds roughly to a Maryland county in terms of population size. Average spending per capita at the canton level in 2003 was about $10,000, or almost double that of Montgomery County, Maryland. However, the size of the legislatures in the cantons ranges from 49 to 180, with an average of over 100. The highest-spending cantons are Zurich, Geneva, and Bern, which have populations comparable to Montgomery County. These had spending per legislator of $76 million, $67 million, and $56 million, respectively. This is almost 90 percent less than what a Montgomery County legislator spends.

In addition, Switzerland has a very comprehensive voter initiative system. Any legislation passed by the Swiss parliament can be challenged through the initiative.

I bring up Switzerland as an illustration of a country in which democracy appears to provide a much better voice for individuals than is possible in the United States. To implement the Swiss fashion of federalism in America would require breaking our country into hundreds of states, probably close to one thousand. Each of these states would have a legislature consisting of dozens of representatives. The point about Switzerland is not that the scale of its governmental units is optimal. However, the fact that Switzerland works at all would seem to suggest that large-scale governmental units, such as the largest counties in the United States, are not necessary in order to have effective government.

Recall the issue of the trade-off between equality and efficiency. It stands to reason that political power is more equal in Switzerland than in the United States. First, there are more legislators in Switzerland involved in allocating a given level of spending. Second, there are fewer constituents per legislator, which would tend to give individual constituents greater opportunities to influence the decisions of their legislators.

A question would be whether the United States enjoys greater efficiency in government relative to Switzerland to offset the greater equality that the Swiss enjoy. To what extent is our public education system more efficient? Our government-provided health care? Our Social Security system? Our public spending on transportation? These would be interesting issues to evaluate.

Within the United States, the relationship between efficiency and scale has been studied for school districts. This literature has been surveyed, for example, by Andrew Coulson. The general finding is that extremely small school districts (under 500 students) are inefficient. However, beyond a relatively modest size (about 2,000 students) economies of scale are close to zero, and perhaps even negative.[14]

The Rich and the Powerful

The rich and the powerful have much in common. Both are sought out by people seeking favors and funding for worthy causes. Both tend to become insulated from the lives of ordinary people. Both seem

---

[14] Andrew J. Coulson, "School District Consolidation, Size and Spending: An Evaluation," Mackinac Center for Public Policy, May, 2007. http://www.mackinac.org/article.aspx?ID=8530

to be driven to increase their advantages, rather than to say, "I have enough." Both seem to regard their close relatives, particularly children, as entitled to inherit their positions.

The wealthy and the powerful can dispose of more resources than they could conceivably consume themselves. Yet, they seek to increase the resources at their disposal. The wealthy and the powerful use their extraordinary resources to benefit their close friends, as well as cherished causes. Being able to choose which friends, relatives, and causes on which to lavish resources is the primary perk of either wealth or power.

Political power and extraordinary wealth allow individuals to control resources that go to worthy causes. People with extraordinary wealth can endow foundations, universities, and other charities. Politicians can allocate taxpayer funds to government programs. Ordinary people with worthy causes, such as medical research or aid to the poor, are beholden to people with wealth or power. As a result, connections to people with wealth or power can in turn be valuable.

People with great wealth can, if they choose, translate that wealth to some extent into political power. Political contributions serve this purpose. Less frequently, the very wealthy will run for office (many politicians have above-average wealth, but few are in the top 10,000 Americans in terms of wealth).

Conversely, political power often translates into personal wealth. One notable example is former President William Clinton, who along with his wife received over $100 million in the eight years after he left office. Clinton's assistant, Rahm Emanuel, earned $18 million in just over two years working as an investment banker after leaving the Administration.[15]

If Bill Clinton represents someone with unusually high charisma, consider instead former Senator Tom Daschle. Nominated by Pres-

---

[15] Nina Easton, "Rahm Emanuel, Pitbull Politician," *Fortune*, September 25, 2006. http://money.cnn.com/2006/09/17/magazines/fortune/politics.fortune/index.htm?postversion=2006091806

ident Obama to be Secretary of Health and Human Services, Daschle had to withdraw in the wake of a scandal involving failure to report income, leading to $128,000 in unpaid taxes. During the controversy, stories came out showing how Daschle's political power translated into economic power. An article in the *New York Times* said that Daschle's fortune

> offers a new window into how Washington works. It shows how in just four years an influential former senator was able to make $5 million and live a lavish lifestyle by dint of his name, connections and knowledge of the town's inner workings.[16]

In terms of wealth, family dynasties appear to be declining. Large inheritances of land do not put someone in the top wealth bracket. Changes in industrial structure and competition within industries make it more difficult for firms to remain at the top for as long as a generation. The largest corporations tend to be publicly held, which means that ownership tends to become diffused and management positions are not passed on to family members.

On the other hand, political dynasties persist. After the 2008 election alone, it was noted that Hillary Clinton was going to be Secretary of State, Caroline Kennedy was under consideration for her Senate seat, the vacated Senate seat of Barack Obama was being sought by Jesse Jackson, Jr., the vacated Senate seat of Vice President Joseph Biden might go to his son, and Interior Secretary Ken Salazar might be replaced in the Senate by his brother. Joining the Senate were Mark and Tom Udall, members of yet another political dynasty. The Senate already included Evan Bayh (son of former Senator Birch Bayh), Elizabeth Dole (wife of former Vice-President Robert Dole), Edward Kennedy (brother of former President John Kennedy), Mark Pryor (son of former Senator David Pryor), and John D. Rockefeller, IV.

---

[16] David D. Kirkpatrick, "In Daschle's Tax Woes, a Peek into Washington," *New York Times*, February 1, 2009. http://www.nytimes.com/2009/02/02/us/politics/02 daschle.html?partner=permalink&exprod=permalink

Winners Take Most

B oth wealth and power seem to be evolving in the direction of win-ners-take-most tournaments, a system in which people compete for a small number of valuable positions. In book publishing, for example, the best-selling book in a year will earn much more than the 1000th-best-selling book. A CEO at a major corporation will earn much more than the average worker.

Income inequality in the United States appears to reflect winners-take-most circumstances. Important industries, such as software and entertainment, involve large bandwagon effects on the demand side and outstanding scale economies on the supply side. The results are that a big winner, such as Microsoft, Google, or a leading popular music group, can achieve outstanding success.

Winners-take-most tournaments may seem fair when skill levels are the most important factor in winning. In chess or tennis, for example, the outcome depends much more on skill than on luck. In popular music, on the other hand, it could be that the best-selling recording artist in any given year is not necessarily more talented than hundreds of musicians who are struggling to make a living in local bars. In addition to talent, there is a great deal of luck involved.

One justification for winners-take-most tournaments is that they may be the best way to encourage individuals to undertake extra effort. This could be the case for bold entrepreneurial enterprises, and it may explain why stock options are a popular form of compensation in such firms. Some types of entrepreneurial enterprises are winners-take-most tournaments. As professor Amar Bhide points out, there is a difference between a "normal" business (such as a restaurant or a nail salon) and a "promising" business that enters a more ambiguous market, such as a biotechnology firm or an innovative Internet company.

The founders of a "normal" business are not entering a winners-take most tournament. They are unable to profit from economies of scale because their labor and materials costs are high. Moreover, they participate in competitive markets where other entrants are plentiful. On the other hand, they do not put hundreds of thousands of dollars of capital at risk.

The founders of a "promising" business sometimes do put hundreds of thousands of dollars at risk. If they are funded by venture capitalists, millions of dollars will be invested. The markets they enter are often winners-take-most tournaments, in which the first company to catch on with the mass market will be highly profitable. Profits tend to increase with scale because labor and materials costs are relatively low.

Even though a great deal of luck is involved in winning the ambitious entrepreneurial tournament, the tournament structure may be justified because of two factors:

1. The losses tend to be borne by the individuals undertaking the risk, both as company founders and as investors. People have a choice about whether to play in the tournament, they know the risk involved, and they understand and accept the consequences of failure.
2. The social benefits of the tournament appear to be high. Much of economic progress comes from entrepreneurial competition.

It would be difficult to reduce the winnings from successful entrepreneurship without altering one of these two factors. Lowering the winnings without reducing losses would tend to reduce the incentive to invest in start-ups, and this in turn would stifle entrepreneurship and slow economic progress. On the other hand, reducing the losses (through a government subsidy, for example) would tend to reduce the incentives for founders and investors to choose their bets carefully.

I am less persuaded that the tournaments used to determine who gets to be the CEO of large, established enterprises work well. These tournaments are supposed to give the CEOs incentives to make good decisions. Perhaps more importantly, the tournaments are supposed to inspire the lower-level executives competing in the tournament to work harder.

I am not convinced that the incentives to make good decisions at the top are really robust. When the economy is strong and the stock market rises, most CEOs are richly rewarded. When the economy is weak and the stock market falls, my sense is that most CEOs are able to blame their company's woes on the external factors. The incentive to *become* a CEO is much stronger than the incentive to perform well as a CEO.

Even if CEOs are only weakly accountable for performance, the tournament could still have some value. It could be that the tournament encourages lower-level executives to work harder and make better corporate decisions as they climb the ladder to the top. The question is whether this system leads to behavior that improves corporate performance or instead merely creates cutthroat competition within the firm, rewarding backstabbing and other dysfunctional forms of office politics.

In fact, the CEO tournament may serve to select traits that are not universally helpful in business. Ruthlessness, arrogance, and sycophancy may be rewarded more than sharing credit or expressing doubt. Looking at the scandals and crises that erupt from time to time in corporate America, it strikes me that egomania is the most common risk factor.

As political power has become more of a winners-take-most game, and as the stakes have risen, the process will tend to select leaders with the same dubious qualities that are selected in the CEO tournament. In fact, there may be fewer forces in the electoral process than in the corporate promotion ladder for mitigating arrogance and ego. The example of Eliot Spitzer comes to mind. Spitzer was known as a crusading reformer, but he alienated many of his peers with his arrogance (he was once quoted as bragging to an opponent that "I'm a ***ing steamroller") before falling victim to a scandal involving a high-priced prostitute.

In the aftermath of the sub-prime mortgage fiasco, it emerged that a number of U.S. Senators and other well-connected political figures had received loans from one of the largest sub-prime lenders on unusually generous terms. The magazine *Portfolio.com* reported,

> Two U.S. senators, two former Cabinet members, and a former ambassador to the United Nations received loans from Countrywide Financial through a little-known program that waived points, lender fees, and company borrowing rules for prominent people...

> Unless they asked, V.I.P. borrowers weren't told exactly how many points were waived on their loans, the former employee says. However, they were typically assured that they were receiving the "Friends of Angelo" discount, and that [CEO Angelo] Mozilo had personally priced their loans.[17]

What struck me about the mortgage loan story is how unexceptional it appeared to the public officials receiving the loans. It did not seem odd to them that the CEO of Countrywide was personally involved in setting the terms of their mortgages, while ordinary borrowers would have their loans priced by lending officers many layers down the corporate ladder.

Mass Media and Mass Politics

Why has concentration of government power increased? This section will look at a number of possible explanations, which are by no means mutually exclusive. However, the emphasis will be on the fit between mass media and mass politics.

One explanation is that increased concentration of government power reflects the natural behavior of political insiders. In this view, it is human nature to seek power over others. Politics is the arena where these conflicts are worked out. Successful political leaders are those who are motivated by the lust for power and are skilled at attaining it.

The United States is not an autocracy. The power of political leaders is checked by competing political forces, both within and between parties. Still, politicians are basically competing with one another *for* power. Enlarging the scope and scale of government is in the interest of all political leaders. Although enhancing government's role only adds to the power of those in office, those who are out of office today can hope to win the next election. Thus, it is easy for leaders of both parties to advocate for and acquiesce to policies that expand government power.

---

[17] Daniel Golden, "Countrywide's Many 'Friends,'" Portfolio.com, June 12, 2008. http://www.portfolio.com/news-markets/top-5/2008/06/12/Countrywide-Loan-Scandal

Another explanation is that concentration of political power is the result of the triumph of progressive ideology, which favors political power. Certainly, in the United States one can discern a long-standing dispute between what might be called the Virginia tradition, a belief in the need to limit government power, and the Massachusetts tradition, a belief that government should be an instrument for reform and progress.

The Virginia tradition includes Thomas Jefferson, James Madison, and many provisions of the Constitution. The Massachusetts tradition includes John Quincy Adams, the anti-slavery movement, the temperance movement, and the women's suffrage movement. Daniel Walker Howe's *What Hath God Wrought* describes America in 1815–1848 in terms that make it clear that the antecedents to modern progressivism can be seen in that period.

From Jefferson through Barry Goldwater, the Virginia tradition opposed the use of Federal policy to protect the rights of African Americans. It was the Massachusetts tradition that pressed for the abolition of slavery in the nineteenth century and for the ending of "Jim Crow" laws in the twentieth century.

The limited-government tradition opposed central banking, business regulation, and taxpayer-funded investment in transportation infrastructure and education. The progressive tradition pushed for these policies, and in the twentieth century added social insurance to its agenda. One can see the victories of progressive ideology over the past century, particularly since the 1930s.

Another explanation for the concentration of political power is that there has been an increase in the demand for government services. This reflects greater urbanization and higher incomes. As the United States has evolved from a predominantly rural nation to one where more than three-fourths of the people reside in urban areas, our needs have changed. Urban life places high demands on infrastructure for sanitation, transportation, and security. Land use becomes more contentious, because the actions of one property-owner are more likely to affect other owners. These factors should increase the demand for public goods, including regulation.

Urban life also brings strangers into close proximity. The informal and personal norms that regulate conduct within an extended family or small village can no longer govern most interpersonal interactions. Formal authority and written laws are more often required.

To the extent that public goods are normal goods, people will want more of them as their incomes rise. Moreover it may be that public goods are superior goods, so that as incomes go up people want public goods to take up a larger *share* in their consumption baskets. Other things equal, this would lead to larger government as societies become wealthier.

In explaining the increased concentration of government power, we also might allow for accident and evolution. The governmental structure that we have today was not designed. There was an architecture embedded in the Constitution, but over time the structure evolved in an episodic, unsystematic fashion.

Christopher Howard, in *The Welfare State Nobody Knows*, shows how certain programs, such as the mortgage interest deduction, evolved from relatively minor policies into major features of the way that government redistributes income in the United States. The mortgage interest deduction was not introduced as a major middle-class subsidy, but that is what it has become. Similarly, Social Security in the 1930s and the tax treatment of employer-provided health benefits were created under very different demographic and economic circumstances.

Other programs with more grandiose intentions, such as national health insurance or laws to encourage employee ownership of stock, have either not passed or failed to produce dramatic results. Some needs are addressed by multiple programs, while other needs are not addressed well at all. There is little co-ordination across programs, so that some individuals face very high implicit marginal tax rates as they approach income levels where benefits are phased out.

The point Howard makes is that there is a random element in America's social welfare policy. Programs are enacted in a form that reflects the political forces in play at the time. As these programs proceed to interact with economic forces, demographic forces, and later political decisions, they take on a character that can differ considerably from the original vision. The end result is a hodgepodge that no one would have consciously designed.

All of these forces—natural desire for power, ideology, urbanization and wealth, and random evolution—have contributed to the concentration of political power. However, my focus is on another factor, namely mass media. *I contend that mass media, particularly television and radio, are congruent with concentrated power, while the Internet is not.* Therefore, I foresee increased tension between the way that media are evolving and the concentrated political power that is a legacy of the mass media era. I use the term "mass media" to refer to media, notably television and radio, that send information from a central source to many recipients. With mass media, it is easy to be a recipient of information but difficult to become a sender. In contrast, anyone can send information over the Internet.

The phenomenon of mass media began to build late in the nineteenth century, with mass-circulation newspapers. However, the real leaps came in the 1930s with radio and in the 1950s with television. Perhaps it was only coincidence, but the period from the late nineteenth century through the end of the twentieth century was a period in which political power became highly concentrated. The 1930s were the most striking period, in which central governments took much more power than they had previously, obviously in Germany, Italy, and Russia but also in the United States.

Mass media make it easier for leaders to disseminate information to followers. They do not make it easy for ordinary individuals to communicate. In that sense, mass media can easily serve totalitarian purposes.

The Internet may encourage a reduction in the concentration of political power. As a medium, it is more democratic, allowing more people to disseminate information. Internet governance is much less intrusive than ordinary government. The Internet thereby provides an example showing that minimalist government can produce richly rewarding outcomes. Finally, by facilitating collaboration and spontaneous production of public goods, the Internet can enable groups to provide substitutes for the work of centralized government.

The Internet can be thought of as a telephone network, but with a different approach to transmitting messages. The Internet and traditional telephones differ in how they approach messages and connections. With a telephone, once you establish a connection, you maintain that connection until all of your messages are transmitted. With the Internet, your message gets broken into what are called packets. These packets are sent over a variety of connections to their final destination, where they are re-assembled. If you have ever had to wait for a Web page to download, what you are waiting for is many information packets to arrive and be re-assembled on your computer.

As Hal Varian and Jackie MacKie-Mason explained,[18] the Internet has become progressively more efficient relative to ordinary phones. The ordinary telephone system wastes connections. When two parties are connected, for much of the time no information is being transmitted. The communication link is effectively idle, but it must be maintained until we hang up.

With the Internet, connections are only maintained to transmit information packets. Instead, what the Internet requires is computer processing power, in order to break up, route, and re-assemble the information packets. Thirty years ago, this computer processing power was expensive, and the Internet was not economical. Today, the processing power is cheap, so that the Internet has become more economical than ordinary telephone communication.

Of course, the Internet did not get to be what it is today by serving only as an alternative way to make a phone call. The Internet also is an alternative to mass media. Using the telephone, you generally connect with one person at a time. Even conference calls typically involve only a few people. An Internet message can go to one person, as in a phone call, but it also can go to a large audience. On the World Wide Web, in theory a message has the potential to be viewed by everyone with access.

---

[18] See, for example: Hal Varian and Jackie MacKie-Mason, "Some Economics of the Internet," Tenth Michigan Public Utility Conference at Western Michigan University. March 25-27, 1993. http://papers.ssrn.com/sol3/papers.cfm?abstract_id=980788

Where the Internet differs from radio and television is that the cost of sending messages is much lower. With radio or television, one has to obtain a license and build broadcast facilities. With the Internet, no license is required and the only equipment needed is a computer with connection to a service provider. It also turns out that the cost of the Internet "backbone" (the large capacity fiber-optic cables, routers, and so forth) is relatively small on a per-user basis.

The Internet does not lend itself to central control. Many countries have government-funded radio and television broadcasts that enjoy a significant audience share. In a totalitarian regime the state-run radio and television may be the only mass media available. On the Internet, government sites have relatively small audiences, and nowhere does the government enjoy a monopoly.

Censorship is relatively easy in broadcast media. A government can promulgate rules, detect violations, and readily shut down violators. With the Internet, each of these steps is difficult. The government's rules apply only to its own citizens, but the Internet's information flows freely across borders. Violations are costly to detect because the content of Internet messages is not directly observable as they flow across the network. Internet packets are like envelopes that only are opened at their destination. For a third party, intercepting and opening these envelopes is difficult and expensive. The difficulties are magnified by the ability of users to encrypt messages and to disguise their point of origin.

When there were three major television networks in the United States, the content expressed tended to be fairly homogeneous. It was in the interest of each network to try to appeal to the majority of American viewers. When there are many sources of information and entertainment, the content becomes much more diverse. Chris Anderson has dubbed this phenomenon "the long tail." Audiences for books, music, and Web sites tend to follow "power laws." In any given year, the most popular book will sell many more copies than the second-most popular book, which in turn will sell many more copies than the third-most popular book, and so on. The best sellers are the "head" of the distribution, and the many books that sell less than, say, 1,000 copies, are the "tail" of the distribution. Anderson shows that the Internet, by lowering distribution costs, has enabled the long tail to flourish. Whereas a store can only afford to carry the best sellers among books or music recordings, the online equivalents can afford to carry works that only sell a few copies.

The Internet offers an environment in which small, niche markets are served in entertainment. Similarly, in politics, one can find points of view represented on the World Wide Web that are not reflected in political parties. There is a "long tail" of politics that includes socialists, libertarians, greens, and other minor parties and factions thereof.

As people with minority political viewpoints find comradeship and support on the Internet, they express dissatisfaction with mass media and the most popular political viewpoints. The "head" of the political distribution has eroded. The number of people who watch evening news programs or read newspaper columnists is declining. The number of people who use Internet news sites and read Web logs is increasing. Fewer people identify strongly as Democrats or Republicans. More people are unhappy with both parties.

When it comes to books, music, movies, and sources for news and opinion, people take advantage of diverse offerings. The "long tail" phenomenon shows that not everyone is satisfied with mainstream material. However, when it comes to government, everyone has to live with what the mainstream supplies. The Internet has allowed niche demands to be satisfied in media. However, government has not followed suit.

Even among political centrists, there is a concern that government has not kept up with the Internet era. For example, in *Making Public Policy Work*, Elaine C. Kamarck presents a chart tracking poll results from 1958 through 2003 that reveals the percentage of Americans saying that they can trust government "just about always" or "most of the time" has fallen from over 70 percent to less than 40 percent.[19]

---

[19] Elaine C. Kamarck, *End of Government...as We Know It: Making Public Policy Work* (Lynne Rienner Pub, 2007).

Instead of pointing to lack of variety (as the "long tail" argument would suggest), Kamarck argues that the drop in satisfaction reflects disappointment with government service and productivity. She says that in comparison with the past, government has probably become more effective. However, compared with the rapid strides made by private industry in terms of flexibility and customer service, government appears to lag behind.

Kamarck writes (p. 2), "Twentieth-century government conducted its business through the equivalent of the assembly line." Later, she writes (p. 56), "For those raised on twentieth-century government the first response is the instinct to centralize power, decisionmaking, and budget authority." She argues that centralization stifles initiative and puts a focus on internal politics rather than on outcomes. For example, she continues, "A terrorist is most likely to be caught by the cop on the beat and/or the local FBI office, not by someone in the White House arguing over budgets."

Instead, Kamarck proposes three ways to bring government up to date (p. 17). One approach she calls "reinvented government," in which customer service metrics and information technology are used to create "government that is run as much like a private-sector business as possible." A more radical approach she calls "government by network," in which various agencies and non-governmental organizations "are all contracted by a state entity using state money." More radical still is the approach she calls "government by market," in which "the work of government involves few, if any public employees and little or no public money. The government uses state power to create a market that fulfills a public purpose." An example might be a market in pollution permits.

However, Kamarck points out that Congress is poorly positioned to implement operational changes in government:

> In a legislature consumed with appropriating at the expense of
> authorizing, there is simply no room for evaluation of existing
> bureaucratic structures, let alone evaluation of new implemen-
> tation structures that require a higher level of oversight. Com-
> plicating this problem is the severe mismatch between the

organization structures of the executive branch and the committee system of Congress (p. 144).

In my view, as government power becomes more concentrated, the
reforms that Kamarck advocates become more difficult to implement.
Congress and other legislatures are too overwhelmed to oversee innovative organizational strategies. Furthermore, government employees
and contractors with a stake in the old way of doing business have
more power than the diffuse potential beneficiaries of restructuring.

Private industry did not adopt quality initiatives, customer-focused
business processes, and more efficient information technology merely
because it is private. Corporate organizations can be as bureaucratic
and averse to innovation as government. But corporations face competitive pressure. Under the threat of losing business to competitors,
even a bureaucracy can overcome its resistance to innovation.

Internet Governance

The fundamental Internet technology is decentralized. One of the
design characteristics of the Internet is that it is supposed to survive having part of the network knocked out. There is no central switch
point through which all messages must pass. Instead, the packets of
information are relayed in what Ed Krol termed a "Pony Express" fashion.[20] The packets pass through various switching points, known as
routers. Depending on conditions of the network, packets may take
different paths between two endpoints.

Similarly, there is no central government for the Internet. No
agency controls the connections to the Internet or the protocols for
software that use the Internet. The only central agency is ICANN,
which controls the domain name registration system (DNS). The
DNS assigns definitive ownership to Internet domains, such as
hoover.org (the Hoover Institution), stanford.edu (Stanford University), or arnoldkling.com (Arnold Kling). I registered a domain in my
name, which I administer. However, the vast majority of people who

[20] Ed Krol, *The Whole Internet User's Guide & Catalog, Academic Edition.* O'Reilly, 1995.
http://www.amazon.com/Internet-Catalog-Academic-Nutshell-
Handbook/dp/0534506747

use the Internet use domains from corporations or other organizations. Most people do not administer domains, so they do not have even indirect contact with ICANN.

There are thousands of software protocols in use on the Internet. These protocols are like conventions or agreements about how messages will be formatted or how programs will interact. In a sense, protocols constitute the very heart of the Internet. Establishing agreement on software protocols is the main governance challenge for the Internet.

Through much of the history of the Internet, protocols were established by Internet Engineering Task Forces (IETF). Different task forces dealt with different protocols. Membership in an IETF typically consisted of whoever was willing to put in the time and effort to participate. Software engineers with a strong interest in the details of how email is implemented would participate in an IETF related to email.

An IETF often would produce a document called a Request for Comment, or RFC. This would be a draft for a particular protocol. While the draft was circulating, programmers eager to exploit the new specifications often would write software that used the proposed protocol. Thus, the draft often became reality, unless and until a new RFC was issued to supersede it.

I think of the IETFs and RFCs as "just-in-time" government. A task force is formed when there is an overwhelming need to resolve an issue. The task force hammers out a draft agreement on a solution. People try to work with the draft agreement. If nobody is terribly dissatisfied, the agreement sticks and the task force's work has ended. If the agreement leaves major gaps or problems, then the same task force or a new task force keeps plugging away at the issue.

I have long been enamored of the Internet's governance structure. Instead of permanently ensconced officials exercising broad authority, the "just-in-time" approach has task forces form around narrow issues and disband when they no longer are needed.

One reason that there is no permanent Internet government is that the Internet does not have a tax base. The software engineers who work on committees and task forces do so as volunteers. They may work for large companies, such as Google or Microsoft, that often have an interest in how software issues are resolved. Those companies certainly pay employees who represent them on task forces. Or, the task force members may be supported by universities or research institutes. However, without a permanent tax base, the people on the task force have no incentive to try to stay in business after their work is done.

Should government workers be long-tenured and well-paid out of a secure tax base? Or should they be volunteers who only work on problems until they are fixed? The answer probably depends on the nature of the public goods being provided. In general, however, the case for well-paid, long-term employees is rather weak. If short-term volunteers can serve on juries, then they can probably perform many other functions as well. Short-term volunteers have an incentive to solve a problem expeditiously. In contrast, long-term employees have an incentive to perpetuate or expand their role in addressing the problem.

Long-term employees tend to become politically powerful. They control the information flowing to legislators, making it difficult for legislators to constrain their behavior. They also can mobilize politically to elect legislators who vote in their interests. We saw that in Montgomery County, Maryland, one of the few instances where an incumbent defeat took place, the loss came at the hands of the employee unions. Steven Malanga has written extensively on the control that public-employee unions have in our major cities.[21] Crises in pension plans, which loom in many cities and states, can ultimately be traced to excessively generous contracts negotiated with these unions.

Long-term employees use their power to block changes to programs. They also seek to prevent the outsourcing of work to private firms or contractors. The interests of well-paid, long-term government employees are not served by "just-in-time" government. To the extent that public goods can be provided more efficiently by *ad hoc* project teams, analogous to the IETFs, concentrated government is likely to lead to inferior outcomes. Flexibility is more likely to come from the pressure of competition.

---

[21] Steven Malanga, *The New New Left: How American Politics Works Today*. Ivan R. Dee, 2005. http://www.amazon.com/gp/product/1566636442

As the Internet continues to flourish, it demonstrates the virtues of a decentralized system. It exemplifies what political theorist Michael Oakeshott called a "civil association," meaning a group of people who agree on a set of rules of conduct without necessarily having a shared objective. Oakeshott contrasts this type of association with what he calls an "enterprise association," such as a political interest group or a private corporation. An enterprise association has a clear objective.

In sports terminology, one might say that a civil association is a set of league rules and enforcement mechanisms. An enterprise association is a team that plays in the league.

The Internet is a set of software protocols for transmitting information between computers. The most basic protocols are implemented in a communication network consisting of cables and routers (the Internet "backbone") as well as in computers and other devices that connect to the backbone. The Internet facilitates a civil association, in that the protocols and the backbone are agnostic regarding the goals of individual users. Corporations and the many interest groups that use the Internet to communicate are acting as enterprise associations. People have specific objectives when they send email messages or browse Web sites. We do not expect the Internet to favor any individual's objective over that of another individual.

In his book *On Human Conduct*, Oakeshott took the position that government is on firmer moral ground when it acts as a civil association rather than as an enterprise association. Given the ability of government to compel behavior, he pointed out that government policies directed at particular goals effectively force some individuals to work toward ends with which they do not agree.

I embrace the notion of government as a civil association on more pragmatic or utilitarian grounds. I claim that the equality of status that people enjoy on the Internet, in that no individual's ends are favored, makes for more efficient distribution and utilization of information. Imagine instead that the Internet were turned into an enterprise association, with decisions about information dissemination made by a technocratic elite. If that were the case, I conjecture that the Internet would not be nearly as useful or rewarding as it is today. The number of Web sites, the amount of information, and the types of transactions that people could undertake would be a fraction of what we see today if instead a central authority had to commission and approve every new Internet enterprise.

Unfortunately, by structuring government as an enterprise association with power concentrated among a narrow elite, we have created an institution that is the political equivalent of a censored, constrained, and restricted Internet. I believe that in the age of the Internet, the increased concentration of political power will seem increasingly anachronistic.

Alternative Medium for Producing Public Goods

Another way that the Internet can affect our thinking about public goods is by reducing the cost of providing them. This leads people to supply public goods at little or no cost. For example, Preston McAfee, a self-described "right-wing economist," who teaches at the California Institute of Technology has put a free economics textbook on line.[22] In fact, professors in many fields have made lectures notes and research papers available for free on the Web.

Wikipedia is a handy and effective reference tool that is built by volunteers. Clay Shirky (a professor of media at New York University) points out that Wikipedia is produced out of the "cognitive surplus" that arises when people have time to spend that involves neither market work nor passive television-watching. Shirky sees potential for this cognitive surplus to be deployed in many ways that produce public goods.[23]

Web blogs are another example of the use of "cognitive surplus." George Mason University's Tyler Cowen has suggested that reading economics blogs is like eavesdropping at lunchtime discussion among economists.

Many of the problems that government tries to solve are fundamentally problems of information. Consumer protection can be viewed as a problem of evaluating goods and services and disseminating the

[22] R. Preston McAfee, *Introduction to Economic Analysis*. 2006. http://www.introecon.com/
[23] Clay Shirky, "Gin, Television, and Cognitive Surplus," http://www.edge.org/3rd_culture/shirky08/shirky08_index.html

results of those evaluations. Financial regulation can be viewed as an effort to make financial intermediation more trustworthy, an effort that relies considerably on information.

Security and police protection are increasingly information-intensive services. My local community has an email list that is used in part to inform neighbors of break-ins and suspicious activity. Using these communication tools, community members have been able to help police apprehend a number of criminals.

In the wake of the financial crisis of 2008, a cry went up for "greater transparency" and "more accountability." It is likely that experiments taking place on the Internet will provide many of the solutions to meet these needs. For example, the haste with which the economic stimulus was enacted raises concerns about how well the funds will be used. Researchers affiliated with the Mercatus Center at George Mason University created stimuluswatch.org, a Web site that takes a list of projects proposed by local governments for stimulus funding and allows individual citizens to express preferences, make comments, and track progress on the projects.

As I see it, in our age of diffused, specialized information, the Internet is a model of neutral, minimalist government. Our actual government, with its high concentration of power, is an anachronism. The knowledge/power discrepancy contributed to the financialcrisis and produced an ineffectual policy response. In the wake of these developments, it seems perverse to wish to expand government, create even more concentration of power, and exacerbate the discrepancy. Instead, it is better to reform government to make it work more like the decentralized systems of markets and the Internet.

In the next chapter, I propose an approach I call "competitive government." This is a more radical idea than having government create markets. My suggestion is to create a market *for* government. Rather than having centralized officials use markets as a means to an end, a market for government would allow individuals to make choices about the public goods they prefer as well as the means used to provide them.

Chapter 3
Mechanisms for Decentralizing Power

This chapter lays out a menu of institutional reforms that could serve to decentralize power. The reforms are intended to shift the means by which people affect government away from representative democracy and toward household choice, voluntarism, and pluralistic institutions of civil society. The goal is to make government more competitive. If implemented, these reforms would alleviate the knowledge/power discrepancy examined in the previous chapters.

I begin by reviewing some earlier thoughts on the relationship between individual expression in an environment of market competition, where people use "exit," and in representative democracy, where they use "voice." I then turn to a survey of possible reforms.

The proposed reforms would shift power from government to markets. The reason for doing so is pragmatic. I tend to think of people in the elite realms of business and government as motivated at the margin by status. Status-seeking *per se* is a zero-sum game. However, when incentives are well-aligned, third parties benefit from status competition. When the competition for status among business executives leads them to develop innovative products that meet customer needs at reasonable prices, consumers benefit. When competition for status among politicians leads them to develop and implement programs that serve broad interests, ordinary individuals benefit. However, I have less confidence in the competition for votes as a mechanism for turning status competition into a constructive game. I believe that market competition is more robust.

These reforms are conceived to be pragmatic and incremental. Rather than lay out a complete utopian vision for society, I assemble a set of ideas that can be adopted or discarded independently of one another. These ideas are not new or original. The common element is that they move decision-making power away from central government.

In the absence of reform, democratic voting today does not effectively address the increasing concentration of political power. Competitive government has greater potential than other reforms, such as campaign finance reform or term limits, to produce a system that reduces concentration of political power and leads to results that better serve the interests of more people.

Theories of Market Competition and Democracy

In 1956, economist Charles Tiebout made a claim that individuals choose their local government based on its combination of tax and spending policies.[1] This theory treats constituents as if they were shoppers in a competitive market for local government services. If true, this hypothesis has some important implications.

First, Tiebout competition forces local governments to be efficient. If two local governments offer the same services, but one government's "price" in terms of taxes is higher, then people will choose (move to) the lower-priced jurisdiction. The inefficient government will lose constituents, just as an inefficient firm loses customers.

Second, Tiebout competition allows diversity in preferences to be satisfied by sorting. Suppose that some people want expensive public goods and are prepared to pay high taxes, while another group prefers lower taxes with less expensive public goods. The two types of con-

---

[1] Charles Tiebout, "A Pure Theory of Local Expenditures," *The Journal of Political Economy* Vol. 64, No. 5 (1956):416-24.

stituents can sort themselves into different jurisdictions, with each group's preferences satisfied by its chosen jurisdiction.

Next, suppose that there are two types of public goods: schools and recreation facilities. Some people might want to spend a lot on both, some might want to spend a lot on schools but not on recreation facilities, some people might want expensive recreation facilities but not expensive schools, and some people might want to spend little on either. If there are enough communities to choose from, everyone can get what they prefer. Taken to the limit, this process can lead to great variety in local government policies.

There are reasons to suspect that the Tiebout equilibrium is not reached in practice. For example, location tends to be sticky because families face high costs of moving. The psychological costs of moving tend to be considerably higher than the financial costs. In fact, large numbers of people, particularly in countries outside the United States, spend their whole lives within a 50-mile radius of where they were born. Moreover, even when people are mobile, the location decision is affected by many factors in addition to the configuration of public goods and taxes. As a result, a family that cares about education for its children might nonetheless end up in a location where schools are not well provided for.

Economist Albert O. Hirschman, in *Exit, Voice, and Loyalty* (1970), described a more realistic situation. Of those who may be dissatisfied with a local government's performance, some may choose to exit, as in the Tiebout model. However, many will instead exercise voice, meaning that they complain about policies and try to get them changed through the political process.

The exit/voice paradigm is quite useful in distinguishing competitive government from democratic government. Competitive government relies on exit to produce change. With competitive government, unresponsive governments lose constituents, in the same way that unresponsive businesses lose customers. Democratic government relies on voice to produce change. With today's high concentration of political power, it is all too easy for government to ignore the public's voice. The massive bailouts undertaken during the financial crisis, despite clear evidence of public opposition, are stark illustrations that the political elites are not moved by voice.

The oldest, and in some ways the purest, theoretical model of competitive government was proposed by entrepreneur Spencer Heath in 1936 in a self-published monograph called *Politics vs. Proprietorship*. Heath evidently was influenced by the single-tax movement of nineteenth-century economist Henry George. The idea of the single tax is to use a tax on land to finance all of government's functions.

Heath reasoned that a land tax was analogous to rent. One can think of government as a landlord, supplying public amenities in exchange for rent. From that perspective, a profit-maximizing landlord might serve just as well as an elected government.

One way to think of the Heath model is that it is the Tiebout model with stronger incentives. That is, under the existing political system, one reason that competition among local governments might not lead to better outcomes in local public goods is that politics may not be consumer-oriented. For example, politicians may respond more to the interests of producers of public goods (government employees) than to the consumers of public goods. Moreover, politicians themselves do not earn higher incomes by satisfying more consumers, which weakens the incentive to try to maximize consumer satisfaction. Changing from a democratic method to a Heath model of ownership would strengthen the incentive to efficiently meet the demand for public goods.

Today, two-thirds of Americans own their own homes, including the land underneath. Public goods are supplied by governments. In Heath's model, everyone would lease their land, and public goods would be supplied by the landlord. Within any given area, there would be many landlords competing for tenants. Each subdivision might have a different landlord. The landlord would decide on rent, amenities, and rules. Tenants would lease the land. Heath's grandson, Spencer Heath MacCallum describes this as "manorialism."[2] He sees

[2] Spencer MacCallum, "The Quickening of Social Evolution: Perspectives on Proprietary (Entrepreneurial) Communities," *The Independent Review* Vol. II, No. 2 (Fall 1997):287–302. http://home.arcor.de/danneskjoeld/F/E/T/SocialEvo.html

manorialism as a voluntary relationship between tenants and landlord (whereas feudalism is a system where the tenant/serf cannot leave without the landlord's permission).

Historically, Americans have viewed tenancy with disdain. We associate home ownership with freedom and equality, while we associate tenancy with serfdom. Thomas Jefferson wanted a nation of yeoman farmers.

In the 160 years between the American Revolution and Heath's monograph, a number of things changed. In 1776, less than 10 percent of the population was urban. Land was the primary source of wealth and a major focus of economic activity. Recall that George Washington was a surveyor. He and many of his contemporaries were land speculators. For over 100 years after the nation was founded, the opening of new lands to white settlers was a major impetus of financial, economic, and political activity.

By 1936, almost half the American population was urban. Physical capital was becoming the dominant form of wealth, and speculation in corporate securities was at least as important as speculation in land. Today, more than three-fourths of the population is urban. Moreover, it is intangible capital (education, skills, social capital, and the quality of private and public institutions) that makes up the largest share of wealth in the U.S. and other developed economies.

In 1776, a system in which the vast majority of people rented from a small landlord class would necessarily have been highly stratified. It would have meant the sort of aristocracy that most Americans wanted to leave behind. But by 1936, ownership of land was no longer necessary or sufficient for attaining wealth and status in our society.

In modern America, a tenant need not be poor and dependent. This is particularly so when one considers that in principle a tenant could own the improvements on the land where he or she lives. Only the land itself needs to be leased. The individual can be free to build a mansion and to sell that mansion to a new tenant.

Although they do not call it rent, many American homeowners pay monthly fees that are used to pay for collective amenities. Neighborhood associations, including condominium associations, manage these funds. Robert H. Nelson points out that "about 50 percent of new housing built in the United States during the 1980s and 1990s was located in a neighborhood association."[3] Thus, many American homeowners are familiar with the phenomenon of fee-based collective amenities. However, the managers of the neighborhood associations typically are democratically elected. They are not owner-landlords.

In commercial real estate, one finds an even closer implementation of the Heath model. A shopping mall or multi-tenant office building will include public amenities, such as parking facilities, that are managed by the landlord. Businesses will lease, rather than own, their spaces within the commercial development.

We are familiar with the terms "gated community" and "private security guard." These phenomena remind us that a very basic function of government is to provide security, including a judicial process for enforcing rules and for resolving disputes peacefully. In *The Machinery of Freedom*, libertarian David D. Friedman devotes considerable effort to arguing that security and dispute resolution services can be provided competitively by market firms. He and other libertarian anarchists believe that as long as government has a monopoly on security, leaders will use that monopoly as a wedge to enlarge government's role in other areas. Thus, the anarcho-capitalists would argue that the sorts of reforms that I will be advocating later cannot be put into place until the monopoly on security has been broken and a competitive model of security emerges. Instead, my assumption is that if people come to share the view that competitive government is better than democracy, then competitive government can be implemented in areas other than security, even if security continues to be supplied in monopolistic fashion.

Most recently, economists Bruno Frey and Reinar Eichenberger have proposed what they call functional, overlapping, and competing jurisdictions (FOCJ).[4] In Frey's *Happiness*, the concept is not moti-

---

[3] Robert H. Nelson, *Private Neighborhoods and the Transformation of Local Government* (Urban Institute Press, 2005), 28.

[4] Bruno Frey and Reiner Eichenberger, *The New Democratic Federalism for Europe: Functional, Overlapping, and Competing Jurisdictions* (Edward Elgar Pub, 2002).

vated by purely libertarian reasoning.[5] Instead, Frey argues that happiness research shows that people are more satisfied with diffusion of political power than with concentrated political power.

With FOCJ, a governmental unit is defined not by territory, but by its function or functions. There might be an elementary education unit, a fire protection unit, a garbage collection unit, and so forth. The territories of these different units could overlap. The fire protection unit serving my house could have a different territory from the garbage collection unit serving my house.

Taxes and regulations would be issued by the functional units, and there would be competition among functional units. My family, or a group of families in my neighborhood, could choose to subscribe to any of a number of garbage collection units, for example. If we were not satisfied with the service of one unit, we could exit by choosing a different unit.

Before moving on, it probably would be worthwhile to make clear the distinction between competitive government and the privatization of government services. With privatization of government services, government officials still make the key decisions: whether to provide the service, how to collect taxes for the service, how much to budget for the service, and who will provide the service. Individuals are supposed to influence these decisions by using voice. They have very little scope for exit.

With competitive government, individuals have no voice (unless the supplier offers a formal complaint mechanism to its customers), but they have many options for exit. The market gives individuals the ability to select from a variety of governing bodies, which in turn will give individuals a lot of choice about which services they want and approximately how much they are willing to pay for them.

The focus of this chapter is not on whether or how to make government perfectly competitive. Instead, my goal is to spell out mechanisms by which government services could be provided more competitively than they are today. There are a variety of such mecha-

---

[5] Bruno Frey, *Happiness: A Revolution in Economics* (The MIT Press, 2008).

nisms, including vouchers, charters, decentralized budget allocation, and competitive regulation.

Vouchers

Vouchers are government transfer payments that can be used only for specific purposes. The most successful voucher program, in terms of political popularity, is food stamps. On a means-tested basis, families receive income transfers that can only be used for approved food products. Within the food category, recipients enjoy considerable choice in terms of what to buy.

The most controversial realm for vouchers is in K–12 education. Proponents argue that school choice allows education to benefit from market forces. Parents using vouchers can reward good schools and put pressure on bad schools either to improve or go out of existence.

Opponents of vouchers raise a number of objections. In Hirschman's model, we can expect fewer parents to exercise voice under a voucher system. That is, once we make it easy for dissatisfied parents to exit from bad schools, they will not agitate for change at those schools. Loss of their voice will hurt those families whose parents are less concerned about school quality or less articulate in voicing their concerns. Another objection is that if vouchers were substituted for direct public funds, families will sort themselves along religious, ethnic, or class lines. Under vouchers, opponents fear that we will lose diversity in school populations, and instead we will wind up with *de facto* segregation.

Much of the voucher debate concerns their effect on school quality. Proponents claim that vouchers improve school quality, and opponents dispute that view. Schooling is an activity for which quality is difficult to measure, and differences in quality are difficult to detect. Disparities in average test scores often can be explained by disparities in the abilities and backgrounds of different groups of students. Whether via nature or nurture, parents seem to matter more than schools in determining educational outcomes.

Educational researchers note a paucity of good experimental evidence. For example, Robert Slavin pointed out that only a handful of articles published in the *American Educational Research Journal* from 2000 through 2003 involved randomized experiments.[6]

My guess is that if significant differences in outcomes were easy to prove, then we would see more educational research reporting such differences. Instead, the state of educational research today suggests that it will be difficult to demonstrate that vouchers make a significant difference in educational outcomes. I suspect that too many factors other than educational methods affect student performance. The research of economist James Heckman and others indicates that success in school can be predicted fairly well by age five, and that few subsequent interventions have large, persistent effects on educational outcomes. On the other hand, I find it plausible that with increased use of vouchers we might see greater efficiency in education. That is, we might see little or no change in outcomes, but spending and costs might be reduced. Of course, that would depend on the size of the voucher.

In higher education, we see the effects of competition at work, but there is scant evidence that this improves quality. A classic paper by Stacy Berg Dale and Alan B. Krueger found that "students who attended more selective colleges earned about the same as students of seemingly comparable ability who attended less selective schools."[7] In higher education, it seems to me that the consumers (parents) are very focused on school reputation. That is, they do not seem to be concerned with the findings of Dale and Krueger. It could be that affluent parents have a strong preference for sending their children to colleges that are popular with other affluent parents, in which case high tuition might raise rather than lower demand.

I worry that an open-choice voucher system could have a similar effect on K–12 education. Affluent parents may be eager to put their

---

[6] Robert Slavin, "Education Research Can and Must Address 'What Works' Questions," *Educational Researcher* Vol. 33, No. 1 (2004): 27–28. http://www.aera.net/uploadedFiles/Journals_and_Publications/Journals/Educational_Researcher/Volume_33_No_1/ERv33n1_SLAVIN.pdf

[7] Stacy Dale and Alan Krueger, "Estimating the Payoff to Attending a More Selective College: An Application of Selection on Observables and Unobservables," *Quarterly Journal of Economics* Vol. 117, No. 4 (2002): 1491–1527.

children in schools with affluent peers and keep them out of schools with large numbers of poor students. This could create a tendency toward segregation, perhaps with tuition playing a sorting role. That is, parents might actually *prefer* high-tuition schools, thinking that other parents who pay the tuition will have children who make for better peers. I sometimes think that this is how elite colleges are able to raise tuition year after year. Higher tuition reinforces the exclusiveness of the elite schools, which in turn reinforces parents' willingness to pay higher tuition.

On the other hand, a voucher system might not be worse in terms of segregation than our existing system. Today, affluent parents can sort themselves into communities with other affluent parents. If that is not sufficient, they can send their children to private schools. Perhaps vouchers, particularly if they were means-tested, would improve school access for non-affluent children compared with what they have today.

I do believe that a competitive market in education would do better at weeding out bad teachers. It also probably would be less prone to expand administrative overhead. (In December of 2006, a local newspaper reported figures for the Montgomery County school budget. There were 138,000 students, and over 21,800 employees, or fewer than 6.5 students per employee. I can assure you that average class size was more than three times that. Given that average compensation per employee was over \$80,000 per year, it seems likely that the bulk of non-teaching staff were not cafeteria workers or janitors.)

However, given my concerns about segregation equilibrium and my doubts about the evidence that schooling interventions are effective, I am not among those who see vouchers as a panacea for education. Ultimately, vouchers would not radically change the situation that exists today. As it stands now, affluent parents are much more effective in using exit (by moving to affluent neighborhoods or by choosing private schools) than they are at using voice in affecting education. Vouchers would enhance the exit option for middle-class parents and provide an exit option for poor parents. But I would predict only modest improvements as a result.

On the other hand, vouchers have considerable potential in the two largest components of U.S. government spending: health care and retirement savings.

Health care spending in the United States is well known to be on an unsustainable path. Both the reports of the Medicare Trustees and the Congressional Budget Office show Medicare absorbing an ever-increasing share of GDP, so that 50 years from now the taxes required to pay for Medicare will be greater than anything that has been sustained in any economy before.

The problems are twofold. The lesser problem is demographic. People are living longer, requiring more late-stage care (a death from Alzheimer's tends to be preceded by far more health care spending than a death from a heart attack), and having fewer children. All of this puts pressure on Medicare and Medicaid (the latter pays for many nursing home patients).

The greater problem is economic. With fee-for-service reimbursement and generous insurance coverage, neither doctors nor patients have an incentive to limit the use of medical procedures. The result is that spending per beneficiary is rising faster than overall GDP. Extrapolating this trend forward, the Congressional Budget Office calculated that health care, which today absorbs close to 20 percent of national income, would by 2082 absorb 100 percent of national income! Clearly, something has to give.

One possibility is that government will institute centralized control over the use of medical services. However, it is unlikely that Americans would be comfortable with health care rationing. I think it is more likely that the government will guarantee payment for health care services that are necessary to preserve life or to treat injuries, but that government funding for other services will be limited. Diagnostic tests, optional treatments, heroic late-stage medical procedures, and treatments for non-life-threatening ailments might become the responsibility of the consumer to purchase. Government's role for these discretionary medical services would be limited to providing a voucher, which consumers could use to purchase health insurance plans or to meet deductibles and co-payments.

The advantage of a health care voucher over the existing Medicare reimbursement system is that it would enable the government to control its health care budget. Under reimbursement, the government ultimately has little choice but to pay for the ever-increasing utilization of health care services by the elderly. Reimbursement represents an open-ended commitment by the government to pay for any and all medical services.

With a voucher system, government could escape the obligation to reimburse all medical services. (Again, fee-for-service reimbursement might be retained for treatments for life-threatening illnesses or for injuries.) Instead, consumers would pay using their own funds, supplemented by vouchers and by insurance purchased using vouchers. The government could limit the growth in vouchers to the growth in tax revenue. If the government only wants to spend five percent of GDP on discretionary health care for people over age 65, then it can issue only that amount in vouchers each year. If consumers want to continue to spend an increasing proportion of GDP on medical services that have high costs and low benefits, they will have to do so out of their own incomes, not through the government program.

Given the unsustainability of the current system and Americans' distaste for rationing, I believe it is highly likely that some sort of voucher system will replace part or all of Medicare and Medicaid. Medical care vouchers may not be a widely-discussed option today, but they are bound to become more prominent in policy debates over the next decade. America may, following the Churchillian jest, try everything else first, but eventually we are likely to find that vouchers are the right thing to do.

The other area where vouchers may be needed in order to achieve fiscal sustainability is in retirement benefits. The question is whether defined-benefit pension plans can work.

A defined-benefit pension plan is supplied to individuals by an employer or by Social Security as it is currently structured. What a defined-benefit plan provides is a lifetime annuity regardless of whether the individual's contributions to the pension plan are sufficient to support that annuity. In contrast, a defined-contribution pension plan provides only the benefits that are consistent with the individual's contributions.

In saving for retirement, an individual faces two risks. One risk is investment risk. If an individual makes investments that produce poor returns, the retirement funds will be disappointing. The other risk is actuarial risk. People who live longer than expected may outlive their retirement savings.

Actuarial risk may be mitigated by purchasing an annuity. If someone reaches retirement age with, say, $500,000 in savings, that person could purchase an annuity through an insurance company. The insurance company will pay out a steady annual income until the person dies. If the person dies relatively soon, the insurance company comes out ahead. If the person lives longer than expected, then the insurance company may end up paying out more than the original savings could support. Averaged over a large number of people, the insurance company's net actuarial risk is small. Individuals enjoy the insurance company's protection against actuarial risk.

Investment risk is not so readily insured. If I knew that my retirement savings were insured regardless of what losses I might take on investments, then I would have an incentive to take enormous risks. If the risks pay off, then I do well. If the risks do poorly, then the insurer will make good the losses. In practice, defined-benefit pension plans often take excessive risks. In the case of private firms, these risks are borne by the government, through the Pension Benefit Guaranty Corporation. This agency may well be bankrupt as of this writing. It is very likely to require a taxpayer bailout. Similarly, state and local defined-benefit pension plans, which were not even fully funded before the market crash of 2008, are badly under-funded today. It is likely that significant Federal tax dollars will be needed to restore the balance sheets of state and local governments.

Social Security does not incur investment risk. That is because Social Security taxes are not invested at all. They are paid to beneficiaries. Until this point, taxes have exceeded benefits, and excess revenues have been spent on other government programs. This excess spending is tracked in an account called the Social Security Trust Fund, which can be thought of as a collection of IOUs from the rest of the Federal government to Social Security recipients.

Within a few years, Social Security benefits will start to exceed tax revenues, and the government will have to make good on its IOUs. Later this century, depending on how demographic and productivity trends play out, the Trust Fund will be exhausted, and the government will have to raise additional taxes to pay for Social Security benefits.

Both Social Security and defined-contribution pension plans will suffer in a weak economy. In the case of defined-contribution pension plans, stock prices will decline and individuals who are heavily invested in stocks will suffer. In the case of Social Security, a weak economy will reduce tax revenues. This will force the government to borrow to pay for Social Security benefits. At some point, if it promises too much and the economy is too weak, Social Security could face a very large deficit.

An alternative to Social Security would be private accounts. These could be thought of as savings vouchers. Individuals would be given funds that they would be required to put into savings. The result would be to increase the risk to the individual of making an investment that works poorly. It would decrease the risk that the government mismanages the Social Security system.

Given the way that state and local governments have failed to keep their pension plans on an actuarially sound basis, I am not sure that I would want to take the risk that Social Security will be properly managed. I personally would prefer a voucher system. If others would prefer government-guaranteed accounts, then it would be easy enough to direct their voucher funds into inflation-indexed government bonds.

Social Service Vouchers

Like all families, low-income families may require a variety of social services to address substance-abuse, legal, marital, or debt problems. Marvin Olasky has proposed giving low-income families generic vouchers to obtain social services.[8] This would give these families

---

[8] Marvin Olasky, *Renewing American Compassion: How Compassion for the Needy Can Turn Ordinary Citizens Into Heroes* (Regnery Publishing, 1997).

choices along two dimensions. First, they would be able to decide which social services are most valuable to them. Second, it would allow them to choose among different providers, rather than be restricted to the personnel and programs imposed on them by government.

Social service vouchers would be more flexible than single-need vouchers like food stamps or education vouchers. However, they would be more regulated than pure cash transfers. With food stamps, low-income families are able to shop in the same stores and choose from among the same groceries as everyone else. They are not limited to second-class food. With social service vouchers, these families would not be relegated to second-class treatment by bureaucratic agencies. They could obtain professional service from law firms, counseling firms, substance-abuse treatment programs, and other service providers.

Charters, Secession, and Opt-out Provisions

Neighborhoods and other groups ought to be able to create alternative governmental units to provide public services. I call these "charter governments," based on the analogy with charter schools.

Charter schools are privately operated schools that are eligible for public funding so that entrepreneurial educators can set up schools outside the government-run system. Charter schools are supposed to serve the same purpose and educate the same clientele as public schools, and are regulated by local authorities. However, they are not managed by government officials, and their staffs are not employees of the government.

A charter community would be a group of people who collectively obtain a service, such as garbage collection, street maintenance, or snow removal. Typically, the group would consist of property owners in a contiguous neighborhood. For charter communities to create competition with large government units, there have to be provisions that permit a chartered community to be formed, including provisions for the fair redistribution of taxes. When a neighborhood adopts a charter under which it will provide, say, garbage collection, households in that neighborhood should be relieved of the taxes that they otherwise would have to pay to obtain garbage collection services from the larger jurisdiction.

The organizational infrastructure for charter communities already exists. There are quasi-governmental structures in place, usually called homeowners' associations, in many housing developments and condominiums. They usually claim jurisdiction over common areas and over decisions that affect neighborhood aesthetics. Often, they provide for common services, such as swimming pools, elevators, landscaping, and security.

Robert Nelson, a scholar who has studied this phenomenon, writes that "There are now more than 250,000 neighborhood associations in the United States, about ten times the number of general-purpose municipalities."[9] Forty years earlier, there probably were fewer than 1,000 private neighborhood associations.[10] As of 2004, Nelson estimates that 17 percent of the U.S. population lives within the jurisdiction of a private neighborhood association.[11] Almost all of these private neighborhood associations were created when the housing units were first built, and Nelson suggests that existing neighborhoods should have a mechanism for forming private neighborhood associations.

Nelson also suggests that the mechanism for creating a private neighborhood association in an existing neighborhood ought to involve five steps. First, a large segment of individual property owners within a proposed jurisdiction for a neighborhood association would apply to become a private neighborhood association. Second, a state body would certify that the boundaries for the association are reasonable and that its proposed constitution and by-laws meet standards of fairness. Third, a committee of representatives from the neighborhood would negotiate an agreement to transfer services (such as garbage collection) from the existing government to the private neighborhood association. Fourth, an election would be held among members of the

[9] Nelson, *Private Neighborhoods.*

[10] "It Takes a Private Neighborhood to Make a Local Revolution," The Urban Institute. http://www.urban.org/publications/900822.html

[11] Robert Nelson, "The Private Neighborhood," Cato Institute. http://www.cato.org/pubs/regulation/regv27n2/v27n2-5.pdf

proposed neighborhood association. If the results of this election are sufficiently favorable (Nelson proposes that at least 70 percent of existing homeowners, representing at least 80 percent of property value, should have to approve in order to form the association), then all residents within the boundaries would be required to join the association. Finally, the existing government would transfer appropriate responsibilities, including land use regulation, to the association.

The complexity of this procedure is due to the fact that a neighborhood association created after the establishment of a neighborhood raises awkward problems relative to the rights of individual homeowners. When a neighborhood association is formed as part of the process of selling an initial housing development, it can be argued that an owner voluntarily chooses to join the housing association by purchasing a home in the development. However, forming a neighborhood association in an existing neighborhood that previously had no such association represents a form of after-the-fact coercion of those who do not wish to have a private neighborhood association imposed on them.

The problem of forming a neighborhood association is somewhat analogous to the problem of forming a labor union. Suppose that a majority of workers at a company wish to form a labor union, but a minority does not want to participate in a union. Because it is not practical to exclude non-participants from the benefits of the union, it is not practical to satisfy both groups. Either the majority's wishes will be thwarted or the minority's rights will be infringed. The procedures for forming neighborhood associations need to try to balance these competing interests.

In order to make it possible to form charter communities, we might need something analogous to the National Labor Relations Board to oversee the process. However, the oversight could be at a state level rather than at the national level. Each state might have a charter community relations board that certifies petitions for charter communities, verifies that the proposed charters are sufficiently democratic, arbitrates with existing governments, and oversees elections within neighborhoods.

The job of arbitrating with existing governments will be important. For example, suppose that a neighborhood tries to break from a municipality for garbage collection service. The municipality will be tempted to minimize the tax reduction that it gives the neighborhood as compensation for not having to collect garbage in that neighborhood. The charter community relations board would ensure that a reasonable price is set.

Another role of the charter community relations board would be to protect minority rights within a neighborhood. If forming a neighborhood association disadvantages a particular homeowner or group of homeowners, the board could act as an arbiter in determining appropriate compensation.

Consider this thought experiment: Suppose that in Montgomery County, Maryland, which has nearly one million people, a charter community relations board drew up boundaries that broke the county into one thousand neighborhoods. At that point, each neighborhood could vote on whether to form a neighborhood association with powers to regulate land use and select municipal services. If the neighborhood chooses not to form an association, it defaults to the County for government services.

Continuing the thought experiment: Suppose that the charter community relations board were to set a price for County services, such as snow removal, road maintenance for residential side streets, fire protection, police protection, and so forth. Neighborhoods where there are private associations could choose which services to obtain through the County and which to obtain from independent contractors. For services that they obtain independently, residents of neighborhood associations would be entitled to reductions in taxes, based on the prices set by the board.

An ideal to work toward would be a system that allows neighborhood associations to partner with one another on a flexible basis. My neighborhood might partner with a nearby neighborhood for trash collection, but not for snow removal.

Today, in Montgomery County, Maryland, the decisions about neighborhood government services for nearly one million people are made by a central County Council consisting of nine members.

Under a decentralized system, hundreds of neighborhood associations would make these decisions.

Competitive Regulation

Nelson points out that neighborhood associations represent another layer of regulation, and they frequently impose more restrictions than general-purpose governments. Nelson writes that "most private neighborhood associations operate in a way that significantly curtails individual freedom. Paradoxically, many millions of Americans have chosen of their own free will to live in a local regime of less freedom."[12]

In fact, the phenomenon of nongovernmental regulation is widespread. Individuals and businesses agree to obey rules and conform to standards in a variety of ways. A private school might have a code of conduct that covers standards of dress or use of drugs. A bed-and-breakfast tries to meet all the standards to be given "four stars" by the rating service.

One example of competitive regulation is kosher certification. Observant Jews only wish to eat food prepared according to Jewish laws. The labeling of restaurants and food products as kosher is undertaken by private agencies. According to the Web site www.hechshers.info, there are over 650 different kosher symbols, which means that there are that many competitors providing certification. Not all of these agencies are equally respected by all Jewish groups. Some Jews will buy food certified as kosher by only a limited set of organizations, rather than accepting any of the 650.

Competitive regulation could be applied in a number of other areas, particularly that of licensing. For example, instead of having a city or county issue restaurant licenses, there could be private licensing agencies. Some consumers might prefer restaurants licensed by a particular agency, based on the rules and standards of that agency. Other consumers might prefer a different agency, and many consumers would be willing to go to restaurants certified by various agencies.

[12] Nelson, "The Private Neighborhood."

Under competitive regulation, issues such as trans fats could be regulated by private licensing agencies. If you decide that you want to avoid trans fats, you can only eat at restaurants that get their certifications from agencies that regulate trans fats.

Competitive regulation could make a particularly large difference with respect to occupational licensing. Many occupations, from physician to manicurist, require state licenses. Often, these serve to create professional cartels. The consumer, rather than being protected, suffers from high cost and screening that is based solely on credentials, not on competence. With private licensing agencies, a better outcome might be realized.

The Internet has produced a number of reputation systems, which can serve as an alternative to regulation. Google's algorithm for ranking search findings is one example. It is based in part on the number of links to a page—an indicator of that page's reputation. The auction site eBay allows buyers and sellers to rate one another, with those rankings made available to other buyers and sellers.

The Internet also makes it easy for people to discover reputations. When someone is interested in a new product or a new service provider, an Internet search can be used to quickly obtain descriptions and reviews.

Another example of private regulation is the credit card industry. Credit card companies regulate merchants by setting standards that merchants must meet in order for credit card companies to process their transactions. Credit card companies also filter transactions for potential fraud.

Private regulation can be flawed—the performance of the credit rating agencies comes to mind. There is a strong incentive for businesses to try to "game" reputation systems. If the proprietors of a system do not take steps to revise and improve their systems, the quality of the recommendations will degrade. It is safe to surmise, for example, that Google has had to alter its system for ranking Web pages for searches in response to the attempts by Web site operators to game the system.

Competitive regulation will not always work better than government regulation. For example, private regulation of air pollution is unlikely to be effective. However, there are other areas (again, occupational licensing is a primary example) where government could get out of the regulation business without hurting consumers because private solutions would emerge.

Direct Budget Allocation

Suppose that Treasury Secretary Paulson had not been able to persuade Congress to allocate $700 billion for a financial sector bailout. One alternative might have been for the Treasury Secretary to appeal directly to the public. He could have gone on television, explained the need for funds, and in the manner of a telethon, solicited donations from individuals. If there are 140 million households in the country, then he needed about $5,000 per household.

In fact, the average contribution that each household would have offered probably would have been less than $5,000. Much less, in fact. What should we make of the discrepancy between what people would have willingly contributed to a bailout fund and what they were forced to contribute through legislation? Clearly, Secretary Paulson and Congress exercised enormous power over the people. Perhaps this is justified, based on popular ignorance of their best interests. Alternatively, it may represent the sort of concentration of political power that ought to be curbed.

In general, I think it would be better if government had to operate more like a private charity. That is, when politicians identify worthy causes, they should have to solicit donations rather than be able to allocate funds by fiat.

One argument against running government programs as charities is that public goods pose a "free-rider" problem. If I can get public services without paying for them, I have no incentive to donate to them. That is why it makes sense for taxes to be coercive rather than voluntary. Funding with taxation does not eliminate all free-rider problems. Instead, it sets up a system in which interest groups try to take advantage of the availability of other people's money.

In 2008, the portion of a typical individual retirement account that was invested in stocks would have lost more than one-third of its value, on average. The defined-benefit pension plans of state and local governments, which were already underfunded, lost similar amounts. However, the manager and beneficiaries of government pension programs suffer no adverse consequences from their losses. They were investing other people's money. The lost funds will be restored by taxes, including contributions from the Federal government.

The beneficiaries and managers of defined-benefit pension plans that are bailed out by taxpayers are free riders. They impose costs on others that they do not have to bear themselves.

Funding all of government with coercive taxation is not the only way to try to address the free-rider problem associated with public goods. There are less extreme ways to increase the incentive for people to make charitable contributions. One way to substitute charitable giving for legislative allocation of budgets would be to designate tax revenues as matching funds for private charities. Individuals would influence where tax money is spent by choosing where to spend their own money. The matching program would provide an incentive for people to donate. As long as you get some satisfaction from donating to a cause, your incentive to contribute increases when your contributions are matched.

For example, suppose that a community currently collects $4 billion in taxes and spends that much on public services. As an alternative, the community could collect $2 billion in taxes, which it will use as matching grants for individual donations to government programs. If the public donates $100 million to the police department, then the police department will receive a matching grant of $100 million from the tax pool. If the public donates $50 million to courts, then the courts will receive a matching grant of $50 million from the tax pool.

In theory, there would be no need for legislators to allocate any revenues. Instead, legislators would provide individuals with a list of programs or charities that are eligible for government matching. Legislators would set tax rates and determine the matching rate. If taxes yield $3 billion in revenues and individuals donate $1 billion to eligible programs, then the match rate would be three for one. If donations tend to be high, then tax rates and match rates may be low. If donations tend to be low, then tax rates and match rates will have to be set higher. Legislators will have the power to assess this balance, but they will not have the power to fund specific programs.

One potential flaw in the donation-based system is that citizens might fail to support some services that arc absolutely necessary. Perhaps no one will donate to support the administrative services needed to fund elections, collect taxes, and administer the matching program. In that case, legislators would reserve some tax revenues to support these baseline activities. Of course, legislators would be tempted to broaden the definition of baseline activities in order to increase their power to allocate funds.

Another potential problem with using a donation-based system to allocate funds for public purposes is that the allocations would reflect the preferences of the largest donors. If the richest citizen in the community likes art, then the community could spend most of its money on art museums.

This problem can be overcome by having the matching amounts vary based on the wealth of individual donors. Donations from low-wealth individual would be matched at a higher rate than donations from high-wealth individuals. The very poor could be given tax credits that they might use to make donations. In that way, everyone would have influence over public spending. Even without donation-based government, Marvin Olasky has suggested giving low-income individuals tax credits to be used for charitable donations.

Under this progressive donation system, the wealthy would pay relatively more in taxes and their donations would be matched at a lower rate. The less-wealthy would pay relatively less in taxes and their donations would be matched at a higher rate. A family's influence over public spending would be proportional to its donations, but the progressive system would compensate for differences in the capacity to donate.

A donation-based system would put government programs under much closer scrutiny. Those who champion and implement programs would have to be able to demonstrate to donors that the programs are worthy and effective.

Under the current system of government, the amount of public spending is determined by legislators. Under a donation-based system, the amount of public spending would depend on the level of donations. Perhaps a compromise between the two approaches would be to have legislators set a minimum donation level, based on family wealth. This would be comparable to establishing a tax rate, but with the revenues allocated by the taxpayers rather than by the legislators.

One objection to taxpayer allocation of revenues is that legislators have more time and expertise to bring to bear. However, in practice, legislators are too busy and the variety of programs is too great for the programs to receive scrutiny. For example, consider the 2009 stimulus bill, which allocated $800 billion and could not possibly have been read by any legislator before it was passed. If individuals were donating their own money to fund programs, they would become interested in the performance of those programs. Today, there are independent organizations that publish evaluations of charities. If government programs were funded by donations, we would see considerable expansion in the charity-evaluation field. Rating services would provide information and guidance to families trying to determine where to give their donations. As a result, spending decisions might very well be better informed under a donation system than under the current system.

Donation-funded public spending can be compared with direct democracy. With direct democracy, people would vote on government spending. There are many conceivable mechanisms for how this would work. One approach would be for budgets to be drafted according to the usual process, but submitted to voters rather than to legislators. Such an approach would raise a number of concerns, because people would have little incentive to evaluate programs in detail.

On the other hand, direct democracy could be implemented in a way that gives individuals the incentive to make careful choices. For example, the ballot might list all programs, and each voter could be given his or her share of the overall budget to allocate. If there are one million voters and a $4 billion budget, then each person has $4000 to allocate among the programs of the voter's choice. This version of direct democracy would be much closer to the donation-based model, in that it would give voters an incentive to obtain information about the effectiveness of individual programs. This in turn would put pressure on program champions and implementers to produce results.

Alternatives to Winners-Take-Most

An economy in which there is considerable income inequality can be termed "winners take most." Other things being equal, winners-take-most seems like an undesirable characteristic. However, it is difficult to change the economy and hold other things equal. If we want people to respond to gluts and shortages according to the laws of supply and demand, then we need to allow prices to provide signals and incentives to change behavior. If we want the economic process to sift through ideas to discover useful innovations while discarding flawed ideas and outmoded practices, we need to allow market incentives to operate.

In the realm of politics and government, the typical citizen has almost no political power. Instead, politicians and technocrats compete to acquire positions that allow them to exercise enormous power over budgets and regulations. We have allowed government to become a winners-take-most system, with very high stakes.

The point of this chapter is that there are plausible alternatives to winners-take-most for dealing with budgets and regulation. For budgets, we could use donation-based systems to give individuals more authority over government spending. We could use vouchers to enable the recipients of government benefits to exercise more choice over how they obtain services. For regulation, we could allow more decisions to be made by neighborhood associations and by nongovernmental groups. There is no need for power to be concentrated as heavily with the few as we have in today's winners-take-most governmental institutions.

The winners-take-most nature of representative democracy makes for compelling theater and spectacle. In 2008, CNN branded its campaign coverage as "Ballot Bowl 2008," an indication of the parallels with that great American football spectacle, the Super Bowl. However, we might be better off if elections were less spectacular. Using other mechanisms to provide public goods, we can give ordinary individuals more power, while reducing the concentration of power among government officials. Most importantly, we can reduce the knowledge/power discrepancy by creating a dispersion of power that better fits with the increasing dispersion of knowledge.

Conclusion

The purpose of this book is to raise the issue of the distribution of power relative to the distribution of knowledge. The discrepancy between diffuse knowledge and concentrated power is becoming an increasingly important phenomenon in our age.

In Chapter 1, I described the role of the knowledge/power discrepancy in creating the current financial crisis of 2008. Managers of financial institutions had the power to make decisions without the knowledge to make them wisely. Regulators also had considerable power, which they used inadvertently to encourage many of the most unsound practices.

In Chapter 2, I summarized trends leading to a diffusion of knowledge and to a concentration of political power. Scientific and technical progress is creating greater technical knowledge and specialization of profession. Meanwhile, political jurisdictions are experiencing scale creep (more citizens per jurisdiction and hence per legislator) and scope creep (government taking on more functions). This is leading to greater concentration of political power.

In Chapter 3, I offered a variety of mechanisms that might be used to reverse the concentration of political power. If enough people become convinced that something ought to be done to diffuse political power, then such mechanisms might be implemented.

The political climate in the wake of the financial crisis instead favors greater concentration of political power. Early in 2009, Congress enacted major legislation under the rubric of economic stimulus. Although this was treated as an emergency measure, the legislation will have lasting effects on the relationship between Washington and state and local entities, as well as between the private sector and government.

In testimony before the House Budget Committee, Alice Rivlin, a Brookings Institution economist and former budget director for President Clinton, said,

> I believe an important distinction should be made between a
> short-term 'anti-recession package' (a.k.a. 'stimulus') and a
> more permanent shift of resources into public investment in
> future growth. We need both.[1]

Rivlin went on to argue that the "more permanent shift" into public investment should be enacted in legislation that was separate from the stimulus package. This would have allowed for more careful deliberation as well as making clear the necessity of allocating revenues to pay for the increased spending. However, her suggestions went unheeded.

In the realm of finance, the failure of the Wall Street elite to prudently manage the funds entrusted to it might have led to a rejection of the idea of giving a narrow elite control over so much wealth. Instead, the address of the elite changed from Wall Street to Washington, under the rubric of "rescue plans" by the Treasury and "quantitative easing" by the Federal Reserve. The Fed expanded its balance sheet to include mortgage securities and other risky assets, while the Treasury went about purchasing preferred stock and other financial instruments from troubled banks.

The political elites have increased public indebtedness at a rate not seen since World War II, if then. State and local pension funds, which were under-funded even when the stock market was booming, were under water by hundreds of billions of dollars in the wake of the

[1] "Budget Policy Challenges," Testimony before the House Committee on the Budget, January 27, 2009. http://www.brookings.edu/testimony/2009/0127_budget_rivlin.aspx

market decline. The state of California was so strapped for cash that tax refund checks had to be delayed. Hundreds of billions of dollars in the "stimulus" bill were directed at shoring up the dire finances of state and local governments, shifting the debt burden to the Federal government. The prospect loomed of a $2 trillion Federal Budget deficit in 2009, with no prospect in sight for returning to a sustainable relationship between revenues and expenditures.

Reflecting the new structure of the economy, a parade of industry representatives came to Washington to plead their respective cases. Automobile manufacturers, university presidents, motion picture studios, and even pornographers appealed for relief from hard times. The only group lacking for lobbyists was the future generations of taxpayers who will have to foot the bill for the surge in spending.

As wards of the state, the executives of troubled financial institutions had to seek permission from bureaucrats to pay dividends or bonuses. Conspicuous corporate consumption, such as paying for naming rights to sports stadiums, had to be curtailed.

Congress, far from feeling chastened by the failures of Freddie Mac and Fannie Mae, continued to pressure financial institutions to respond to political considerations. Congressmen cajoled banks to lend, and the "stimulus" legislation included provisions designed to force down mortgage interest rates, even though these rates had already fallen to record lows.

The push for a large fiscal stimulus was made without regard to changes that have taken place in the economy over the past 50 years. Claudia Goldin and Lawrence Katz, in *The Race between Education and Technology*, present data showing that in 1950 more than four-fifths of the labor force had a high school education or less. As of 1970, this proportion was still more than two-thirds. Today, less than one-third of the labor force has only a high school education or less. With this more highly skilled, heterogeneous work force, it is far from clear that spending directed from Washington, DC will be able to re-employ workers who have lost their jobs. Instead, this spending may merely serve to increase demand in sectors where full employment already exists.

If my reading of the trends is correct, then this dramatic increase in concentrated government power is out of step with the diffusion of information. The financial bailouts and fiscal stimulus are likely to end badly, if not catastrophically. One dire scenario would be for foreign investors to start to demand a risk premium for holding United States government securities. If anything could cause the financial "freeze-up" that policymakers worry about, a loss of confidence in the United States government as an institution capable of repaying its debts would do so. The elite in Washington are showing remarkable alacrity in their willingness to risk such a debacle.

Diffuse information can best be used by decentralized processes, such as the market. Markets can fail to produce good outcomes; however, just because markets sometimes fail it does not follow that government will always succeed. There are circumstances under which information problems are difficult to solve.

At the moment, the political stars are aligned to favor greater concentration of government power. However, I doubt that this political trend will be able to overcome the structural trend of greater diffusion of information.

Perhaps I am wrong. Perhaps what appears to me to be a high concentration of political power is mitigated by forces that I have overlooked. Or perhaps I am misreading the technological trends, and in fact new information and communication systems give the advantage to central planning, so that people will benefit by outsourcing more decision-making to government technocrats.

In any case, people should be thinking about the knowledge/power discrepancy. I hope others will try to examine the extent of this discrepancy and the trends toward diffusion of knowledge and concentration of power.

I do not claim to have settled the issue of what, if anything, should be done about concentrated political power. My hope is that this book will help provoke further discussion of this neglected but crucial topic.

Acknowledgements

Peter Berkowitz of the Hoover Institution first proposed this project, and he provided considerable help and encouragement along the way. Hoover's editorial staff provided very efficient and helpful support. I am grateful to them and to the Hoover Institution for the opportunity to present these ideas.

Index